Become Your Own *Beloved*

A GUIDE TO DELIGHTING IN SELF-CONNECTION

LEE HARRINGTON

A TWIN FLAME BOOK
ISBN: 978-1-63758-903-8
ISBN (eBook): 978-1-63758-904-5

Become Your Own Beloved:
A Guide to Delighting in Self-Connection
© 2023 by Lee Harrington
All Rights Reserved

Cover design by Hampton Lamoureux

Although every effort has been made to ensure that the personal and professional advice present within this book is useful and appropriate, the author and publisher do not assume and hereby disclaim any liability to any person, business, or organization choosing to employ the guidance offered in this book.

No part of this book may be reproduced, stored in a retrieval system, or transmitted by any means without the written permission of the author and publisher.

Post Hill Press
New York • Nashville
posthillpress.com

Published in the United States of America
1 2 3 4 5 6 7 8 9 10

To Bonnie, who taught me self-love through farmers markets and having the perfect chair

Contents

Foreword 9

Introduction: A Long, Strange Partnership 13
Chapter 1: Hello, Old Friend: Meeting Yourself Anew 23
Chapter 2: Table for One: Going on a First Date.............32
Chapter 3: Getting to Know You: Deepening
                Self-Knowledge 44
Chapter 4: More Than Words: Examining Your Labels 57
Chapter 5: Deserving Delight: Understanding Love
                and Connection 71
Chapter 6: Dancing with Yourself: Exploring Sensuality ... 93
Chapter 7: I Me Wed: Making Commitments................110
Chapter 8: Please Forgive Me: Moving Past the Past 123
Chapter 9: The Juggling Act: Balancing Other
                Relationships 136
Chapter 10: You Are Not Alone: Tapping into
                 Community Support......................................149
Chapter 11: Maintenance Needs: Keeping Up with
                 Comfort and Care..164
Chapter 12: Welcome Home: Being Your Own
                 Beloved for Life...180

Acknowledgments...184
About the Author 187

Foreword

More than fifty years ago, in the early days of my feminism, it was a great revelation to me that I could have a self. I had been raised Roman Catholic and taught that the greatest virtue, particularly for women, was a selfless devotion to husband and family. Selfless: it was against the rules for me to even *have* a self, much less care about my self, and it was definitely not about me seeking my own destiny. I am forever grateful to my young, rebellious spirit for pronouncing a decided "No!" to everybody else's ideas about who I should or could be and charging forward to clear my own way toward discovering my self and learning to love her.

It was a pretty stormy voyage of discovery. I had fought my way out of a physically violent relationship, six months pregnant with ten bucks in my pocket. Everything I am today started in those difficult and joyous days. It wasn't that hard having next to no money—it was easier being poor back then: we always had a roof over our heads, good food to eat, and quite nice clothes from the thrift stores. I gathered community around me in the form of other post-Summer-of-Love single moms and had lots of support, love, noisy kids, and wonderful lentil stews for thrift-store-costumed dinners. "It's Edwardian for dinner tonight!" I would sing up the stairs, and we'd all get into our falling-apart silks and corsets and celebrate beauty in our very own ways. I am deeply grateful for all the housemates, mothers, and kids I lived with communally in the first five years of my daughter's life.

Revelation number two: I didn't have to find a husband to lead a happy and secure life. I had been a young adult in New York City before I came out to San Francisco in the Great Migration of 1967. Back east, back then, a woman's status and thus my status was determined by the status of my male partner, not by my own achievements or any intrinsic value. I vowed to discover a sense of security inside myself that I owned and operated. To that end, I decided to remain unpartnered for at least five years, to find out who I was when I wasn't struggling to become somebody's wife. I also vowed never to be monogamous again, which is how I wound up almost thirty years later creating, with my beloved co-author Janet Hardy, *The Ethical Slut: A Practical Guide to Polyamory, Open Relationships, and Other Freedoms in Sex and Love*. I still keep these vows.

In the early seventies, following the work of Masters and Johnson, there was a lot of exploration into what healthy and rewarding sex would look like, and how we would get there. Sexual "problems" were studied, and it was learned that most were not the result of deep psychological disturbance (often not seen in any other part of a person's life) but rather from lack of permission, approval, and opportunities to learn. One interesting truth emerged: one place you could always practice expanding your sexual abilities was when you were having sex with yourself. Right, masturbation. Once we accepted that sex with ourselves was healthy and normal and morally just fine, thank you, the possibilities of practicing new sexual delights in the privacy of our own bedrooms or bathtubs offered a rich field for learning how to have happy, satisfying, and even loving sex. With yourself. For me, that meant no more "Some day my prince will come and so will I." (I owe that quote to an unknown sex therapist from the 1970s. If that's you, please email me. I would love to connect with you and cite you properly.)

It was a new world. I had struggled with orgasms in sex with partners, men and women, non-binary and trans, with only occasional success. Now I owned my orgasms, and I got to choose to share them with my partners! It was a very new world. Eventually I realized that sexuality was my path, that I would do whatever I could to heal the old wounds and share discoveries of new pathways toward being a strong and independent person with a lot of love to share, with myself and with a lot of other lovely people. I shared my discoveries with everybody who wanted to listen, which has led to a marvelous life that I get to share with friends and lovers and co-parents and, indeed, my wonderful co-author. We have five books in print together, and I have been blessed to be able to share my hard-won independence with the world and get love back for it.

Now Lee Harrington has given us a book about their journey to their own personal and rewarding truths, with lots of ideas and practices about how anyone wanting to make changes in their lives, in the direction of developing a strong and supportive relationship with their own sweet Selves, can learn to do so. This is true whether you are on the early steps toward liking yourself, or you are ready to dress in your Saturday night best, take yourself out to a fine dinner, and come home to have wild passionate sex with yourself. Lee's exploration of self-learning and self-loving becomes a tool that, like my own journey with self-connection, can help you find the core of who your *Self* is.

So read on, Gentle Reader, and I hope you find ideas and practices you can use to discover and explore and strengthen your relationship with yourself. Here's one hint from me: if you seek compassion in your life, and ways to open your heart to others, start by opening your heart to yourself. This may feel scary, it may indeed be scary, but the practice of self-love, self-acceptance, self-support, and self-compassion can heal a lot of old wounds and lead to wonderful freedoms in life.

Lee says: "You deserve love and care, affection, and attention. Love is there, in your being, waiting to be expressed by you, for you. Let's start the conversation, and meet your journey-mate, your partner, your beloved." Let this book show you how to discover yourself in all the facets of your brilliant diamond being.

So read on, Dear Friends. This book is for you.

Dossie Easton
Marriage and family therapist
Coauthor with Janet W. Hardy of *The Ethical Slut*
Written in the mountains north of San Francisco

Introduction

A LONG, STRANGE PARTNERSHIP

I've known my partner for a long time.

I've known them since they were born, perhaps before. I was there when they scraped their knee for the first time and when they had their first kiss. I laughed out loud when they listened to hilarious jokes and curled up like a ball when heartbreak came. My heart swelled with pride when they got great grades against all odds, and I took long walks with them when they needed to think. Heartache, colds, fears, joy, delight, loss, delicious meals, perfect sunsets—I've been there for it all.

My partner, my beloved, myself.

We have each known ourselves our whole life, but many of us don't really have an awareness of who we are. At the core—our *Self*. The Self, in the context of this work, is the many faces of who we are. It includes the longings we have that are often unconscious thanks to a culture that has given us an unhealthy relationship with our bodies, our desires, and our authentic experiences in this world. The Self is who we are when we peel back our assigned identities from the world around us and find who we are inside.

> True self-care is not salt baths and chocolate cake, it is making the choice to build a life you don't need to regularly escape from. —BRIANNA WIEST

My own path toward becoming my own beloved has taken me on a journey to meet myself, greet myself, and form a deep relationship with myself. It took me a long way to get there, and I get to know myself more all the time. Why is this so important? Because there have been large swathes of my life when I didn't know myself and, more than that, didn't like myself. Both things led me to make choices I might not have otherwise, many of them toxic choices. Both also took away chances to be fully present with the beautiful being I have come to learn that I am.

So many of us spend more time getting to know other people and their desires than we do getting to know ourselves. We say things to ourselves that we would never let another person say to us. We treat our bodies in ways that we'd never treat anyone else. Why? Because when we don't know someone, even if that someone is ourselves, it's easier to ignore their needs, wants, dreams, and desires. It is time that each of us got to know our Self.

Amid a deep emotional journey, I came to realize that I didn't really know me. Parts of what I did know, I didn't like. As with partnerships and friendships with others, I had a chance to expand through getting to know myself, even if this can take time.

Whether I like it or not, I am with this person for life. This person called *me*. I wake up with them every morning, go to work with them, surf the internet with them, hang out with other friends or family with them, and go to sleep in their skin every night. It hit me that I couldn't afford to dislike this stranger, because they would always be there. Always. I couldn't run away from or avoid them. They were in the mirror every time I brushed my teeth. Eventually I would have to talk with them.

So, the process began with conversations, and then going out for dates. Yes, dates. Instead of saying I'd see that movie when it came out online because no one else wanted to go with me, I empowered myself to take me out, complete with popcorn, because I deserve to be spoiled as much as anyone else. I took tables for one at my favorite restaurants, not because no one wanted to go with me, but because I enjoy good food. Because it was time with me.

The concept of being my own beloved came from a friend who had married themself. They had made a deep vow to care for themself, for better or worse, for richer or poorer, in sickness and in health. It was profound and felt right. I realized how many people I'd put before me, how many relationships I'd clung to because we live in a culture that says someone else completes us.

Our meta-culture, the unconscious reality that surrounds us and that we rarely notice, is obsessed with people being in relationships. It is a Cult of the Couple. This cult has devout worshippers who fall upon the sword of their own delight to follow the tenets of that cult. The Cult of the Couple says that we are incomplete without another person. It says this person is not just our other half, but in some sects, that they are our better half.

We live in a culture that says we as individuals are not enough. We need the other half to be whole. Not just that, but those who are in this unconscious cultural cult feel profound pity for those without a partner. "Someday you'll find the right person." "They'll come around eventually." "It's a shame; you two were so great together." "Oh, poor thing, you must be so lonely."

There is a difference between being alone and being lonely. I know a great number of people who have romantic or life partners but feel very lonely, even when that other person is around. Beyond this, the story that we must be coupled to have value even stops some individuals from leaving unhealthy or abusive partnerships. Telling people that you are sorry to hear they got divorced disempowers people who finally left an abuser or a situation where they were profoundly unhappy.

There will always be people who don't believe in you. Don't be one of them yourself. —Mat Auryn

People who consciously choose to not be partnered are embracing a truly alternative relationship structure. They are the ones who have the courage to say that they are enough, that they love themselves, that they choose to be fully present with themselves and all that they are.

This book is not here to advocate for people not to be in relationships with others. Not at all. In fact, there is a chapter on exactly that topic, as well as a chapter about how our health and well-being is embedded in community health and well-being. This book and its practices are about the process of loving yourself—getting to know yourself, connecting with yourself, and loving yourself. By doing so, we learn the skills to make a conscious choice around how we know, connect with, and love others.

As human beings, we do not exist in a void, and this book does not aim to show otherwise. We can explore these skills and experiments while partnered with others, because for some of us, having the support of other people can help us have the confidence to build a relationship with ourselves. This book is not explicitly for single, partnered, or multi-partnered individuals. It is for people. People like you.

Some will look at this project and see it as a profound experiment in narcissism. Others may be concerned that the externalizing language that encourages inward reflection is a form of psychological dissociation. My hope is that the language used is simply a way to understand the concept of self-knowledge and self-love, because so many of us have an awareness of how to get to know and love others. We are applying those concepts on ourselves, and the language in this text allows us to dig into that idea. If you experience schizophrenia, dissociative identity disorder, various other personality disorders, or struggle with boundaries around how to perceive your sense of identity, consider consulting with a helping professional before engaging with the exercises in this book.

Various self-help gurus make glib statements that you need to "learn to like you" and "be your own best friend." But just like saying people should learn to communicate, it's rarely explained how to do so. You know what? Learning to like you can be harder than it sounds. It was for me at least. After years of conscious self-exploration, I'm still figuring out the shape of this internal friendship every day.

> On my own path in self-love, self-delight, and conscious self-exploration, I made the decision to marry myself, just as my friend had. Part profound act of self-love, part wound-healing, part spiritual journey, part performance art—I bought myself an engagement ring. I had five one-word vows I wanted to share with myself when I eventually got married engraved on the inside of it.
>
> It sat on my desk for months.
>
> Why? I was convinced that I might say no. It was an existential crisis of self-love. I knew that there were parts of me that weren't ready for that leap. Rationally I know I was already "death do us part" with myself, but having a commitment to me was too much. It was too scary.
>
> Eventually I popped the question on a pier just beyond the Mahatma Gandhi statue in San Francisco. When I got married, I took myself out into the woods alone at an outdoor

event that people I cared about were also attending. I had a mirror in hand and said my vows to the reflection before me. Back with the group, I ate cake with all my friends.

Being married to myself hasn't been easy. I've been married to me for years, and I still struggle with having a spouse who says cruel things to me or who wants to run away from time to time. I dance with others, knowing that this internal love so deeply fuels my love with the other people in my life, but I still realize I need to take time to self-connect. I forget sometimes and wonder why I feel so burnt out. It's because my partner, myself, needs me.

Loving yourself does not mean you cannot love others, or that you need to isolate away from the world. However, if you consciously choose to give yourself space away from the world, that is your prerogative. I have no interest in holding you back from your authentic Self, whatever that looks like. After all, this world needs a revolution and evolution of authenticity.

Authenticity helps us choose what is best for us, in each moment, at our core, to help us be healthy, happy, and whole. Coming from a place of authenticity, we become empowered to meet others at every level in our lives as powerful beings whole and unto ourselves. We come to see them as whole and unto themselves as well. This may seem easy enough, but authenticity can be a complex topic, and is explored throughout the book, especially in chapter 9. Instead of coming from a place of desperation to friendships and relationships, in coming from a place of authenticity, we see another person's authenticity and want to connect—whole being to whole being. We come not to "fall" in love, losing our balance, but to "rise" in love.

Finding ourselves is an ongoing process. After all, each of us evolves, every day. We learn new things, acquire new scars (both physical and otherwise), find new passions, and embrace new joys. We have a chance to keep meeting ourselves anew. That is the beauty of this work. It is the opportunity to keep saying hello to the person we see each day in the mirror.

Each chapter in this book features an exercise at the end to help you on your quest. Each of these exercises provides tools for the adventure. Some will call to you, and others may not. Each exercise also features adaptations for people with different life realities or disabilities, so please look after each exercise in case the adaptations work better for you.

Stop acting so small.
You are the universe in ecstatic motion. —Rumi

Some of the concepts and exercises in this book will be easy for you, and others might be a struggle. That is not just okay; it is normal. In doing the work in this book, some practices that I thought would be simple turned out to be difficult, and ones I expected to push me were a breeze. I keep surprising myself.

There are multiple ways to navigate this text:

- Read the text from start to end as a collection of thoughts, to be inspired and add new ideas to your journey.
- Read the text, and then go back and do the exercises in order, to have the overarching concepts in hand before diving in.
- Read one chapter at a time, and then do each exercise before moving forward, to have the exercises build on each other.
- Flip through the table of contents and read just the chapters that call to you.

There is no "right" way to explore this text…because this is *your* journey. There will be some that will inspire you, and others you will want to disengage from. The exercises range in length from five minutes to a month in length, so skipping some for time or partially doing them may be more accessible for individuals with busy schedules. Undoubtedly, along your path, you will find your own exercises, experiments, bumps, lessons, and projects to undertake. Fantastic! That means that you are doing the work. You are learning more about yourself.

Mine is just one journey. Yours lies ahead.

It is time to find and connect more deeply with your partner, your beloved, yourself.

Yours in Passion and Soul,

Lee Harrington
March 2023
Denver, Colorado

Chapter 1

HELLO, OLD FRIEND: MEETING YOURSELF ANEW

When we meet someone new in our lives, we tend to ask questions. What is your name? What are your hobbies? Where do you work? Who do you live with? Do you have kids?

Through simple questions, we start exploring the person before us. We assess if we have things in common with them and if we have similar perspectives on life. Through their answers, we see if we share political or religious beliefs, and whether we are likely to get along.

Success is liking yourself, liking what you do, and liking how you do it. —MAYA ANGELOU

With those we haven't seen in a while, we tend to ask for a life update. How has it been going? Where are you living nowadays? What have you been up to recently? What are you currently excited about? Do you have any upcoming plans?

These questions create a chance to fill in the gaps of our knowledge concerning that individual. We find the stepping stones upon which further conversations can take place. They create portals with which to explore their life, gateways into their current state of mind for potential connection.

PROJECTING ON OTHERS AND OURSELVES

What we usually don't notice is that when we meet someone, we are rarely meeting *them*. We are encountering a blank screen upon which we are placing our own projections. If they tell us they are a nurse, we project all our internal stories and history concerning what a nurse is. If they are wearing a tee shirt with a specific sports team on it, we construct a myth about them based on that shirt that may have no relevance to who they are.

The same is true when others meet us. Each person encounters us, and before we open our mouth, a fantasy is being projected upon a cardboard cutout that has our shape. They paint a picture of what it means to have our skin color, wear certain jewelry, or have the gender they perceive. Our answers to questions tell them not just the words we say, but our accent, volume, level of certainty, and the expression on our face.

We are not who they see.

As human beings, we do the same thing in the mirror.

Before we have a chance to ask ourselves, "Who is the being before me?" we have woven a fiction upon that reflection. They look tired, have put on weight, or are too skinny. They look immaculate, appear disheveled, or are too weird. People will like this person; no one will like them. Our eyes stare at the projection, and our mind fills in the blanks in a way that has nothing to do with who we are.

If you make friends with yourself, you will never be alone. —Maxwell Maltz

It's not our fault. Humans have been trained to do this through an evolution in which snap judgments increase the likelihood of survival. For *homo erectus*, when the leaves on the bushes shook, those that did not stop to debate whether it might be a predator lived. Their fast judgment around the likelihood of food having spoiled, or what help a broken limb needed, allowed for the community to thrive. Unfortunately, those snap judgments come with a cost. That cost is knowing others, and knowing ourselves, on a deeper level.

GETTING TO KNOW OURSELVES

We have the capacity to open our minds, hearts, and spirits to see beyond the labels we have stuck to our own skin. We are more than our labels. We are not just mother, brother, worker, student, partner, friend. We are more than our stories of old, young, short, tall, strong, frail. We are more than the questions, labels, and projections that our cultures have taught us should matter. The opportunity exists for asking ourselves questions, sharing our history and dreams, and learning about who we are.

What does this person have a passion for? What do they enjoy or dislike? What struggles do they long to tell someone they trust? What celebratory statements do they want to scream from the rooftop?

In learning the skills of listening to ourselves, we build the capacity to see others beyond our projections of who we think they are as well. Assessing ourselves and opening our minds to possibility, we also get the chance to learn more about ourselves. After all, who else can we share some of our stories with—and more than that, our core Self?

> My maternal grandmother grew up as a Depression Era baby. The youngest of her family, she picked up stories from not just her parents, but each of her older siblings, about how she should move in the world. How she should love. How she should study at school. How she should eat.
>
> One day, at the grocery store, I went with my grandmother to the produce area. She picked up some spinach, took a deep smell of the leafy greens, and put them in her basket. She did the same with a cantaloupe and put it back down. I asked her what she was doing.
>
> My grandmother said she'd grown up desperate for food, and even as an adult she had had times of food scarcity. She

always bought what her family said made the most sense. Then, one day, she went to the grocery store and saw that some of the produce was on sale, and she bought some to eat that day. She found herself asking why she never considered it before. It was because she had been assuming her desires based on family traumas, preferences, and habits.

From then onward, when she had time to go to the grocery store regularly, she ate what her body wanted rather than only getting the boxed food her family had told her was the best option. Her body was happier. It taught me that even in our sixties we can change our relationship with what our family said was the right way to do things, and in doing so become a better friend to ourselves.

Beginning with this dialogue, we create a space to ponder what we like about ourselves, and what we need to navigate within our relationship with ourselves. What are they, your sense of Self, interested in? Does it match what you are doing right now? Sometimes, until we explore these pieces of our life, we don't even realize there is a mismatch—or a perfect match that we didn't notice was already there.

Let's start the conversation, and meet your journey-mate, your partner, your beloved, yourself.

✧ *Exercise: Become Your Pen Pal*

We will start this conversation by literally starting a conversation.

Many of us have lost the art of being a pen pal—writing letters that only one friend or family member will ever read. This is your chance to show the friend you are getting to know that they deserve the time of your written word and the experience of reading those words with fresh eyes when your letter arrives. The friend in this case is you.

Remember: with each of the exercises in this book, you get to choose if and how to engage with them. The choice is always yours.

1. Acquire three to five stamps. A minimum of three is best for the exercise, to really get the conversation going; the longer you connect with your pen pal, the deeper you are likely to share.
2. Find paper and an envelope that suits you. Perhaps the paper will match your envelope, be aesthetically pleasing to your eye, or be torn sheets of lined paper out of a notebook because it's what you had access to. People who prefer to use their computer can type their letter before printing it out.
3. Write an introduction to your pen pal. Tell them about yourself. Who are you? Describe what your journey has been like so far in life. You might choose to write about why you are looking for a pen pal, or about your current biography. There is no wrong answer. Feel free to make it yours, from choice of pen color to

font type, even doodling on the edges of the page or including original art.
4. Once you have written your letter, however long it turned out to be, sign the bottom with a name you want your pen pal to know you by.
5. Slide your letter into the envelope, seal it, and put the stamp in the top right corner. Overly large letters may need additional stamps.
6. Address your envelope to yourself and from yourself.
7. Breathe deeply and drop your letter in a mailbox to go out.

Now, you get to wait. The postal service in each area varies and waiting for your letter is part of the process. This helps you forget the exact details of what was written. Your mindset will change to that of the friend who is about to receive a letter.

8. When your letter arrives, open it, and find a place to read each word. Pretend you don't know what you wrote. The mind tries to fill in the gaps with its expectations. Your pen pal may have written something other than what you are expecting.
9. What do they have to say? How does it make you feel? What surprises you, annoys you, or makes you sad? Does anything make you laugh, find comfort, or shake your head with a sigh?
10. Without judgment, think about what they said. If this were a pen pal you didn't know, what advice might you give? Do you have thoughts and reflections that you want to share?

11. Feel free to start writing back. You might recount your week, share a story, offer advice, or tell them a secret. Are you going to include a funny joke, beautiful poetry, newspaper clippings, printouts of memes, or a recent work story? Remember that you are trying to get to know your pen pal, so think twice before using cruel language that might shut down the discussion, or further wound them if it's a response to their vulnerability.
12. Slide your reply letter into a new envelope, stamp it, address it, and mail it off.
13. Repeat the process until all envelopes and stamps have been used.
14. Thank yourself for doing the work.

Adaptations

For those whose budget does not allow for postage, or whose life does not have the privacy necessary for such an exercise, a journal that no one else has access to offers a similar option. Wait at least two days to read the last entry and write your response.

This exercise can be modified for those who are blind, visually impaired, or dyslexic. Instead of writing a letter, record an audio file or post a private video blog. If posting your files or videos online, make sure to set your settings to "private," as they are only for your connections with your pen pal, yourself. You also can write a private blog, but make sure not to read and edit what you wrote immediately after—this is a special gift to your future Self.

Going Forward

Consider keeping the letters, audio files, or videos you create. They can be fascinating to reflect on once the exercise is complete, even years later. We can learn a lot about how we used to think about things by looking back at a memory box of letters, photos, and other keepsakes. This is just as true with letters to and from yourself.

Chapter 2

TABLE FOR ONE: GOING ON A FIRST DATE

Having started to get to know your partner, yourself, it's time to work up the bravery to take them out on a date.

The Cult of the Couple has developed a wide variety of dating rituals. Some involve asking a person's parents before asking them out. Others include meeting someone online from a sexually explicit personals ad, meeting up for dinner before getting between the sheets, or, in the reverse order, enjoying an erotic liaison before going out for drinks. Many of us feel confusion nowadays about what it means to "date" someone, or what a singular "date" looks like.

A date can mean spending quality time in a quiet conversation or going out for a night on the town. For some, it is a romantic dinner, pulling out the fine china, or ordering their favorite takeaway for a night holed up in front of the television. Perhaps it is tuning in for a digital dance party or watching an online class at the same time and discussing it afterwards. It can be taking the dogs to the local park or going for a motorcycle ride through the countryside. For those who enjoy the arts, visiting museums and galleries can be great ways to spend time with someone, as can taking in a community theater production in person or online.

> You are worth the quiet moment. You are worth the deeper breath. You are worth the time it takes to slow down, be still, and rest.
> —Morgan Harper Nichols

YOU ARE A PRIORITY

In dating yourself, you have a chance to learn to set aside special time with your own company, whether that means spending fifteen minutes literally smelling flowers, going for a long hike in the wilderness, watching an episode of your favorite series, or heading to that concert you've wanted to go to. No excuse is needed—we each deserve "us" time and taking ourselves on a date is a ritualized way to do just that.

How can you best show that you are a priority in your own life? Taking someone on a date says, "I am making time for you, because you matter to me." People rarely do that for themselves. We spend so much time putting work, career, family, friends, and even complete strangers ahead of ourselves, leaving little time, energy, or other resources for ourselves.

Partly, this is because our culture says doing so is greedy, that people should prioritize others before themselves. Parents are told by family and media messages that they should put their dreams on hold to take care of their children. Meanwhile, the world tells others that they should work hard for money to gain material wealth to have resources for others or to show the world that they have value. These kinds of stories leave a person without much space for their core Self. They hand over their energy and time to the "other," risking the possibility of missing out on a large part of life.

By fueling ourselves, and making ourselves into priorities, we often end up with more capacity to give. We cannot feed the world from an empty basket. We feed ourselves so that we can feed others. We create a symbiotic relationship with partners and communities by feeding ourselves, having them feeding themselves, and feeding the web between us all. The personal becomes the communal, while the communal becomes the personal. But, amidst all of this, the personal must be remembered as an essential part of the equation.

> Find what makes your heart sing and create your own music. —MARC ANDERSON

Unfortunately, so many of us try to compensate for our hunger for self-connection in unhealthy ways. We fill the holes in our hearts with overeating, drinking, drugs, obsessive behaviors, compulsive sex, internet addiction, and more. We even try to satisfy our hunger by gouging holes into the hearts of others, hoping that by knocking them down, we can lift ourselves up. None of it works in the long run.

INTROVERT AND EXTROVERT BATTERIES

We start feeding ourselves energetically by meeting our inner Self and spending time with them. In the case of going on a date, we can do this literally. It's important to remember that different people might feed their Self through introversion or extroversion. An extrovert is someone who gets energetically fueled by going out into the world or connecting with others, while an introvert can find themselves drained by doing so. You can also think of this distinction with a battery metaphor: introverts charge their batteries through time *away from* the world, and extroverts charge their batteries through time *in* the world.

If you are an introvert, the idea of going out to dinner at a packed restaurant and asking for a table for one might be horrifying. Instead, taking the time to make that meal at home, set the table, pour a glass, and stay in might be heavenly. For an extrovert, an afternoon music festival might sound delicious, while staying in alone for a day can feel restricting.

Many people have a blend of these two qualities. They are ambiverts. Think of this as having two fuel tanks inside the machine of your spirit. They each fuel up on different things. One tank might be smaller than the other and need less fuel to feel completely full. One might get spent easily and need refilling on a more regular basis. Therefore, some ambiverts that are predominantly extroverted need alone time, because their introvert tank, as small as it might be, needs to be replenished.

Consider this concept when planning time with yourself. Just as people who are dating others choose to stay home on a date or go out on the town on different evenings, so it can be for you. It might even change day to day, in the same way that people dating might choose different dates based on whose needs are being centered on a specific day. Will your self-date be a night out amongst the throng of humanity, or a quiet evening curled up with your favorite book?

> My mother was both an introvert and an extrovert. The introvert part of her loved curling up with a good book in a home she had decorated by herself, for herself. The extrovert loved having deep conversations with friends and interacting with coworkers.
>
> She found a hybrid self-date that worked for her: going to community events. She made a list of every art show, farmer's market, holiday bazaar, and state fair she saw an advertisement for. When she had open time, she would look at the list to see what she had written down and ask herself if going to that event would bring her pleasure or get her out of a negative emotional state she was in. Some of the events were far away, and others nearby.
>
> When she got to the event, she would choose how she interacted with everyone based on which battery needed to be filled. If she was needing extrovert energy, she would talk with every vendor, flirt with artists, and share her own sto-

ries with other attendees. If she was craving introvert time, she would take in the stalls from a distance, window shop, or buy things with a silent nod and then move on. The same exact date could be approached from either lens, bringing her pleasure and joy either way.

WHAT KIND OF DATE DO YOU WANT?

When dating, sometimes we assume that we know someone well enough to tell what type of date they want. Long-term couples, and people who have self-connected for years, often fall into this pattern. Unfortunately, this belief system can sometimes become a life-limiting habit.

Depending on who you are, taking yourself on a date can be a chance to explore new things. Do you want to order from your favorite café again, or have a culinary adventure? Would you find more satisfaction in rewatching movies you know you love, or heading to a local cinema and seeing what is about to start playing at that moment? Neither is good or bad, but this is a chance to look at trends in your life to see if they are limiting habits.

This applies in the other direction as well. If you find yourself using any open time you have as a chance to thrill-seek and try new things, ask yourself whether that is a desire or a habit. Even if you know you are fed by the adrenaline rush, what will happen if you try climbing the same mountain again, this time with the eyes of a returning friend who is bringing their whole sense of Self along for the ride?

Many people don't want to spend time with themselves and unconsciously fill up every moment of every day as an avoidance tactic. One of the reasons is that they don't know how to spend time with themselves. If they don't like themselves, time with themselves can be frustrating—and even painful. This is the reason that this practice is not just an excuse to do something you like; it's an exercise in spending time with your Self.

Unlike dating another person, we can't decide that we don't like them and thus never want to see them again. We are always there. The person we don't like spending time around will be there when we wake up, take a shower, go to school, or visit the grocery store. They are everywhere we are. By practicing spending time with yourself, you create spaces for finding what you like about yourself.

For some, this will be easy. For others, it is a process. Neither answer is "right." It is simply a journey.

Some people have a best friend they once held animosity toward, and it turns out the two people had friction because they were so alike. This can happen within us as well.

> I struggle with mood issues. When I am in the throes of depression, it can feel like I am buried under the weight of reality—that the light of delight is far away. It can even feel like it will never return.
>
> What gets called self-care, as someone with mental health challenges, can require modifying the tools that I use to reach myself. I might not be able to take myself out on a

date when I am depressed, but I can put on music that is neutral rather than music that pulls me into darker places. I might not feel capable of telling myself that I love me, but I can pull out the folder of self-love memes I have saved on my phone and make one of them my lock screen. I might not have access to the energy needed to go out to a museum, but I can make my appointment with my therapist.

Sometimes upkeep of our relationship with ourselves is about the little things, just like any other relationship. If you are the kind of person who struggles with the muddy grey places of the heart, know that you are not alone and that loving yourself in those places does not have to be about grand overtures. It can be about being there for yourself, using the tools you have, and making those tools accessible to where you are today.

✧ Exercise: Take Yourself on a Date

A relationship must start somewhere. For many, it is on the first date. This is your chance to go on yours with an amazing being—you.

Remember: with each of the exercises in this book, you get to choose if and how to engage with them. The choice is always yours.
1. Brainstorm. Start writing down places you have wanted to go or things you have wanted to do. Especially things that others have said are silly or a waste of time! This exercise is about you—your desires. No matter how strange or small something seems, no matter

whether it is something brand new or a secret pleasure you have wanted to enjoy again, write it down with no judgment.
2. Set the list aside and walk away for at least thirty minutes.
3. Figure out a time that can be just for you. For some, this will be thirty minutes after work, and for others, it might be a weekend.
4. Retrieve your list and compare it with the time available. If you know that you only have thirty minutes, but your list is full of day-long treks, this is valuable information. You are craving more time with you, and this can encourage you to look ahead in your schedule and block off time for those experiences to happen. After all, if we don't make something a priority, it is unlikely to happen.
5. Comparing the time with the items on your brainstorm list, see which one rises to the top as being a great opportunity for your first date. Whether it's an extrovert or introvert date does not matter—what matters is that it intrigues you.
6. Take a moment and ask yourself if you'd like to go on a date. Offer what the date would be and that you'd like to go with yourself. You can do this inside your own head, or more literally by saying it out loud.
7. If you say yes, put it on your calendar. If others ask if you have spare time then, say you do not. You have plans. Whether you tell anyone else or not, you have a date. If you say no to the date, give yourself compas-

sion for not being ready for this level of intimacy. If it feels appropriate, you can offer yourself a counter idea that is less involved (for example, watching a movie at home rather than going out and about town), but do not push anything. Any person, yourself included, deserves to have their boundaries acknowledged and not be forced into anything they don't consent to.

8. When the time arises, get ready for your date! If you were going out on a date with anyone else, what would feel good for you to do? Wear a special perfume or cologne? Pull out your favorite hiking equipment? Dress to the nines? Put on your favorite workout clothes? This is your chance to head out on this date with your best foot forward.
9. Be on time. Show yourself the respect you deserve.
10. Head out on your date!
11. If anyone asks if you're waiting for someone, answer with a smile (or other authentic expression) that no, you're here to enjoy some time with yourself. If that feels uncomfortable, feel free to simply say, "No. Thank you." That person is basing the question on the programming of our culture, and they are most likely not invested in your answer. Their question is not really about you.
12. Listen to yourself and your desires during your date. Sick of the movie because it turned out to be a flop? Do you usually white-knuckle through it even if you are suffering? Leave. It is your date. There is no reason to nonconsensually suffer at any point of this process.

In fact, if this whole thing feels ridiculous, feel free to laugh at the situation. It can seem somewhat silly but still be a useful tool for learning to be around yourself.
13. After your date, thank yourself for your time spent.
14. If you enjoyed your time, go ahead, and set a time for a second date!
15. Regardless of how your date turns out or whether you even went on a date at all, thank yourself for putting whatever time and effort into it you did.

Adaptations

For those who live hectic and chaotic lives, putting a date on a calendar may not be realistic, or finding even thirty minutes to spend alone seems unlikely. In these situations, finding time and energy for yourself is still important for feeding your spirit. This is where microdates come in.

Let's say you must get from your job site to the soccer field to pick up your kid before rushing them off to class and… already, it sounds exhausting. On your way from work to the soccer field, drive down a side road instead of the main route you usually take. Look at the land around you, the house styles; you can even put on music you love. Sing along—no one is in the truck, sedan, or minivan but you!

We sometimes find our bliss intertwined with what we give to others, but it is important to still find those threads of authenticity rather than painting "should" upon our spirit. You are not doing anything wrong by not having the time to go on a long date. Instead, take a moment to find a slice of joy that is just for you and embed it in the day. Choose an outfit to wear today based on what gives you joy, have dinner tonight for the whole gang be something you want, or find little moments to breathe and relax.

Going Forward

If you enjoyed your first date, consider making it a regular part of your schedule. This might be a weekly night at home, a monthly excursion, or a yearly retreat. Whatever it might be, blocking it out on your calendar and making yourself a priority is a powerful act. Once it's on your schedule, treat it just like you would treat a date with someone else. If you wouldn't make a date with someone else, the same can be applied to you. Showing up for yourself helps build trust within your relationship with yourself, showing your unconscious mind that you are a priority in your own life.

Chapter 3

GETTING TO KNOW YOU: DEEPENING SELF-KNOWLEDGE

In the early school years, teachers sometimes use basic questions as prompts for writing exercises. They ask children what their favorite color or favorite type of food is. With crayon in hand, students scribble out "green" or "lasagna," focusing more on whether they can create the shapes or spell the words than on the answers themselves.

To be yourself in a world that is constantly trying to make you something else is the greatest accomplishment. —RALPH WALDO EMERSON

As kindergarteners and elementary schoolers, many of us allowed ourselves to answer these questions without judgment. There were no right answers, and our guide in the exercise had told us so. It didn't matter if the person next to us answered "red" or "tacos." No one cared. The exercise was about our own right answer and our own hand scrawling letters across the page.

Growing up, we began hearing that there were right answers for things. Our family, friends, coworkers, and the media all told us that certain colors weren't supposed to be popular. National, regional, and local cultures proclaimed that certain foods were gross. Who could like chartreuse? What sort of person enjoys pickled pigs' feet?

LOCKED IN OUR PAST ANSWERS

Beyond outside judgments, we can also get locked in our past answers. If we tell ourselves repeatedly that we love the color green, where is the space for our fledgling love of the color orange? This is especially true when our previous answers are reflected back to us by our loved ones, who still buy us truffles for every holiday because we once proclaimed our passion for fancy chocolates when we were young.

> My father was a hard man to shop for when I was growing up. I never knew what to buy him. He was great at getting himself everything he needed.
>
> One day, I saw him laughing at some *Dilbert* comics. Suddenly my young mind was elated that I could now find him something when getting him a gift. Every birthday,

> every Father's Day, every Christmas, I got him *Dilbert* material. *Dilbert* ties. *Dilbert* calendars. *Dilbert* comic collections.
>
> Six or seven years later, I was still buying him *Dilbert* presents. Now an adult, I had become stuck in a rut based on a single interaction I had with him. Watching him open a present I realized then that he had been amusing me, not wanting to hurt my feelings. It struck me how long I had done this with him. Over time, I started watching if I was doing this with other people…until years later, I realized I was also stuck in a rut with myself.
>
> When I finally asked myself what I wanted as a holiday gift, both from myself and in updating lists of ideas for friends and family, I ended up with different answers than I had before. I deleted travel books from the list and added resources on theology. I asked Santa not to put chocolate in my stocking and to put in gummy candies or fresh fruit instead. This process took self-reflection that I had not done since I was a child.

As humans who must operate in the world at large, we have become trained to self-edit. To hold on to patterns. Change can scare people. We find comfort in knowing the way of things and having patterns we can rely on. Because of this, asking ourselves whether something is still true can feel destabilizing. It can feel scary.

Asking ourselves the things we think we know about ourselves sounds simple, but it is not for the faint of heart. It takes bravery. We face our assumptions, set them aside, and ask with a willingness to hear what we, today, have to say.

Favorite colors may not seem like a big deal. Why would it matter if you like orange more than green now? Perhaps it doesn't. But when we practice opening ourselves up to the possibility that we don't know what we want, when we let our unconscious mind speak, new answers of all sorts can emerge.

CURATING YOUR WORDS

Whether in a conversation with someone else or in a pen pal letter to ourselves, we curate our words. We pick and choose the language we use. We guard our hearts using the terms and tales we are used to as a shield to protect our vulnerable hearts.

This is why automatic association games at parties are such simple systems, yet intense get-to-know-you tools. These games come in many forms. Perhaps the first person says a word, and the next person in the chain states the next word that comes to mind, before the third person replies to the second. Other forms involve posing single questions and giving folks only a few seconds to reply. Maybe you have played *Mad Libs* or other fill-in-the-blank group games. The varieties are endless.

Many people find such games easier to play with a set of strangers than with people they have established relationships with. When we don't know someone, it can be easier to share our truths because we have nothing invested in that individual. On a blind date or with an online friend we'll never meet in person, if they don't like what we have to say, it doesn't matter. But if we share with a friend or partner that we have an answer they don't know about, if they don't like what we have to say, it can matter.

Remember who you were, before the world tried to tell you who to be. —Dulce Ruby

WHAT ARE YOU LEAVING OUT?

Sometimes, we don't want to answer the questions we have for ourselves. That's okay. In fact, we can learn just as much from the questions we ask ourselves as from the answers.

After all, we do this with other people all the time! There are some people we don't want to share certain intimacies with. Maybe we don't know the person that well. Maybe we think the topics are private. Maybe we don't want to share certain information that day. Maybe we don't know how we feel about the details yet ourselves.

The same is true when answering questions for yourself. There are some questions you don't know the answers to yet. Maybe you will want to journal about the question, or perhaps talk with a friend or therapist about it if you prefer to process it externally rather than internally.

It's possible that you're not ready to hear an answer yet. That is okay too. We each need our own processing time, and questions that seem easy might not be. Your inner Self might also be shielding you in some way, or it might not think the question is relevant to your journey. Be gentle with yourself when getting to know you.

❖ Exercise: Answering Your Self

Just as automatic association is a wonderful party game, it can be an effective tool for setting down your processing shield. Through the act of a gut response, you will get to see a snapshot of where you are at today. The answers you give today may or may not match the answers you give tomorrow. Because of this, do not make radical life changes based on one-time answers without giving yourself space to reflect on those answers again later—letting hours, days, or weeks pass.

This exercise is a chance to get to know yourself better by seeing what the back of your mind has to say. What *you* have to say. Set aside any judgment regarding the answers and just let them be. After all, no one must see these answers but you, and there are no right answers.

If you're listening to this in audiobook form, you can download the written worksheet at http://www.passionandsoul.com/beloved.

Remember: with each of the exercises in this book, you get to choose if and how to engage with them. The choice is always yours.

1. Set aside ten to fifteen minutes for this exercise. If you only have a few minutes here and there, that's okay—just pause the exercise whenever you need to.
2. Acquire a writing utensil that feels good in your hand.
3. Shake out your body. Stretch your arms, wiggle your toes, and let go of the stories and stresses of the day for a moment. This is a moment for you to listen to *you*.
4. Take three deep breaths. With the first, breathe in, and release. With the second, breathe in, and release

with a longer breath out. With the third, take a deep breath, filling up your body from your toes up to your nose, hold for a moment, and release until your shoulders drop. Repeat that last one if needed.
5. Once your shoulders have dropped, begin the worksheet. You don't need to answer the questions in order or even answer all of them. Just read the first question that comes to your attention and then write the first answer that comes to mind. Don't spell it out in your mind; don't memorize it. Just write it. Remember—there is no right answer.
6. Take a breath. Read and reply to the next question.
7. Repeat this exercise until you've answered all the questions or need a break. If you notice that your shoulders have crept up, take a moment to pause, shake your body out, and repeat the breathing step from earlier in the exercise.
8. If you hit a question that your mind does not want to answer, or that you don't have an interest in answering, feel free to skip it. You can either come back to it later or simply know that you are not called to do it at this time. Don't judge yourself or go digging for a "why" at this time.
9. Set the worksheet aside. Stand up, stretch out your body, drink some water, or take some other short, non-stressful break.
10. Once you feel refreshed, read your replies. Do any answers surprise you? Does anything make you smile, or leave you with something to ponder?
11. Thank yourself for doing the work.

Adaptations

If you have dyslexia, dysgraphia, or a vision impairment, or do not enjoy doing writing-based exercises, you can download the audio file at http://www.passionandsoul.com/beloved. Once you've downloaded it, you can answer the questions in a few different ways:

A. Write your answers on paper with your chosen writing instrument.
B. Type your answers out on your computer and save them for later.
C. Audio- or video-record your answers on a smartphone, computer, or other device.
D. Answer out loud.
E. Answer in your head.

I strongly recommend recording your answers in some way, because the mind can be very good at misremembering or shifting an experience. This does not mean you are evading your own answers. You are experiencing something profoundly human. Recording your answers will also allow you to come back and reflect on them if you repeat the exercise a few hours, days, months, or even years later.

Worksheet

What is your favorite color?

_____

What is your favorite food?

_____

What is your favorite song?

_____

What is your favorite movie?

_____

What is your favorite beverage?

_____

What is your favorite animal?

_____

What is your favorite number?

_____

What is your favorite place to visit?

_____

BECOME YOUR OWN BELOVED

What is your favorite chore?

_____

What helps you when you are sad?

_____

What helps you when you are angry?

_____

What is your greatest fear?

_____

What is your greatest hope?

_____

What is something you like about yourself?

_____

What is the most important thing in your life?

_____

When are you happiest?

_____

What helps you feel confident?

_____

What frustrates you?

_____

What are you most proud of yourself for?

_____

What is the hardest thing you have done in your life?

_____

What have you always wanted to try?

_____

Where do you feel safest?

_____

When did you last laugh?

_____

When did you last cry?

_____

BECOME YOUR OWN BELOVED

When did you last scream?

_____

When did you last give it your all?

_____

When did you last fake it?

_____

When did you last do something just for you?

_____

Who are you most inspired by?

_____

What is your dream job?

_____

What are you scared of?

_____

What are you thankful for?

_____

What is your favorite game or sport?

___

What superpower do you wish you had?

___

What helps you feel at ease?

___

Going Forward

Feel free to return to this exercise at any time, allowing yourself each time to answer without any preconceived judgments or thoughts about how you might have answered previously. As the author, I also give you permission to photocopy or print out these pages for your personal use, so that you can return to the exercise as often and wherever you like.

Chapter 4

MORE THAN WORDS: EXAMINING YOUR LABELS

We all carry stories about ourselves. It's very easy to confuse these stories with who we are as people. When someone asks us who we are, many of us respond with our name, career, or where we are from. We might list our family ties and relationships, gender, ethnic or cultural background, religion, orientation, or maybe a hobby. But are any of these things who we really are?

> Defining myself, as opposed to being defined by others, is one of the most difficult challenges I face. —Carol Moseley-Braun

Labels are useful tools for shorthand communication. When getting to know someone, labels allow us to efficiently create constructs of ourselves in the mind of the person before us. If we say we are a dancer, their mind can remember who we are by associating our face and name with those of other dancers they have known or seen in the media. If we mention our faith, they can fill in the blanks about what our ethics, morals, and ways of operating in the world might be based on their understanding of our faith. If we share that we are affiliated with a specific political party, their own political affiliation will subconsciously create a tale of how they should interact with us as an ally, a potential collaborator, a curiosity, or even someone we might experience conflict with.

Some of these labels, stories, constructs, and identities might include:

- Age
- Birthplace
- Current residence locale
- Relationships
- Marriage and/or partnership status
- Family (biological and/or of choice)
- Parenting status
- Sexual and/or romantic orientation
- Race
- Accent
- Ethnicity
- Nationality
- Citizenship status
- Skin color
- Visual aesthetic (hair, makeup, wardrobe)
- Work and/or career (past or current)
- Political affiliations
- Faith, spirituality, and/or religion
- Hobbies

- Physical and/or mental health
- Education level
- Life experiences and/or personal history
- Diet and/or fitness practices
- Ethics
- Specific lifestyle
- Past and/or current incarceration
- Class and/or economic situation
- Resources (financial, time, energy, expertise)
- Sex, gender, and/or gender identity
- Cultural background and/or norms
- Skillsets
- Number of partners and/or lovers
- Kinks and/or sexual practices
- Weaponry ownership
- Fame
- Leadership role
- Physical and/or mental disabilities

SPLIT-SECOND DECISIONS

Everyone fills in blanks about individuals they meet based on their own experiences. However, this means that we sort people and situations into categories, such as friend or foe, positive or negative, and invest in or avoid, without always taking the time to think about it first. Our upbringing hands us the algorithm we use to do this with the people around us. Many of us do not realize how deeply this algorithm is ingrained.

Our self-assessments are affected by this tendency as well. Most of us have internalized certain beliefs from the cultures we grew up in and the world at large, even if they were not directly taught to us. If our culture teaches us that homosexuality is wrong, having lighter skin is more valued, or people with certain accents are not as smart as others, we might carry internalized homophobia, racism, colorism, or bigotry. These internalizations manifest themselves in many ways, most of which we do not become aware of until someone points them out.

These internalizations can even appear deceptively positive! If we learned along our life journey that a specific political group, gender, or religion is superior, we might look at our own self-identity and identify ourselves as being inherently superior. This can be toxic, as internalized superiority removes our opportunity to connect with others and truly examine how we see ourselves. It cuts us off from possibilities, urges us to live up to impossible standards, and causes us to harm others.

We also might be concerned about identifying ourselves as certain identities because we or those around us (directly or culturally) have biases about them. When you are getting to know yourself, it's important to give yourself permission to acknowledge the private thoughts, identities, interests, and realities that are in the back of your mind. Keeping something private and away from others is different than keeping it a secret from yourself. We can all make choices about those private identities and whether we want them known by or seen by others. In the process of becoming your own partner, your own ally, your own friend, your own beloved, opening that hidden cabinet in the back of your mind can be a powerful act.

Growing up, I was one of the white kids in a predominantly Chicano part of town. I was taught to be "color-blind," language that unfortunately meant I wasn't seeing how my neighbors' struggles were different from my own. I rationally knew that some of my neighbors were worrying about immigration issues or having the different experience of speaking English as a second language, but the rhetoric at my schools and from my family made these issues seem like not a big deal.

Whether we claim a label or not, our life journeys are unique. If we don't acknowledge differences, we might not see that our personal journeys affect how we have formed our relationship with ourselves. I saw this with my family's income; other kids at my school had as much money to go shopping as my family paid in rent. These friends had access to activities—ones that some people label as self-love—that I did not. A part of me thought I didn't deserve these things because I did not have access to them.

I saw this difference in experience because it affected me personally. I had not seen that my experience being white meant I did not have certain barriers that my friends who were Black, Indigenous, or other people of color experienced due to racism. We cannot "self-love" our way out of systems of scarcity, oppression, or prejudice. Don't think one expression of self-love is better or worse than another just because it isn't what others experience or have access to.

REFRAMING LABELS

Looking at both your public and private labels allows you to also set them aside and see who you are beyond them! You might start with what you are good at or like about yourself. It might feel like bragging. That's okay! In fact, it's great to have a sense of ego. It can fuel you to live up to who you want to be in this world, as long as you don't let it get out of balance. After all, putting down others is not healthy. However, seeing that you are a positive and powerful individual who can help the world is important.

Perhaps you are a person who does small acts of kindness for others. Maybe you are learning all the time and are great at sharing resources. It might be that you are taking steps in caring for the environment. Gratitude could also be a practice you bring to how you approach the world—doing so even occasionally can change how you interact with others and how they interact with you.

What are some of the ways or time you are awesome? Telling yourself these stories can remind you of the traits you carry. Keeping a storehouse of these times can help you when you're feeling low or need to give yourself a motivational moment.

When you examine yourself, some of your stories might not seem positive. It might feel like you are being hard on yourself. Take a deep breath and reframe that concept! It's important to strive to be the person you will thrive as in the world, to possess the traits that can make you happy, healthy, and whole. You do so when you work toward being the person you want to be, rather than getting caught in the quagmire of self-anger or self-pity.

If we want to get to know someone, we don't just want to know what they do—we want to know who they are. By telling our stories to ourselves, we get to know what we say about ourselves, and start learning who we think we are. This will change over time! We might tell ourselves the same story through an upbeat lens one week, and a more sorrowful lens the next. That is alright.

For me, being a person who cares about my friends is a story I tell myself. Some weeks that's a positive story in my head. I am a joy-bringer, a person who connects with others. Other weeks it is a painful one. I am someone who puts others in front of my own needs. At the end of the day, both are interpretations of the core story I tell myself—I am someone who cares about my friends.

> It takes courage to grow up and become who you truly are. —E. E. CUMMINGS

This is part of the process of building intimacy with someone in our life as well. Some weeks they have lows, some weeks they have highs, and we get to know them across the spectrum of their expressions. Over time we build a deeper understanding of them. By doing so with ourselves we can develop a deeper understanding of ourselves as well.

By hearing and examining your own labels and stories, you can get to the questions and beliefs beyond them. You can begin to understand who you are and learn about that Self.

✧ *Exercise:* Hearing Your Self

When was the last time you shared things about yourself with you? This is your chance! Remember, there are no right answers, and you will undoubtedly have different answers today than if you do this exercise again in a few months. Whether you do this once or many times in the future, listen to what *you* have to say. If you disagree, note that. Some of the labels we carry serve us, and others make us serve them. Some of the stories we tell ourselves hinder us, and some inspire us to be the best we can be.

This is a chance to get to know you better by seeing what the back of your mind has to say. What you have to say. Set aside judgment. No one has to see these answers but you.

If you're listening to this in audiobook form, you can download the written worksheet at http://www.passionandsoul.com/beloved.

Remember: with each of the exercises in this book, you get to choose if and how to engage with them. The choice is always yours.

Set aside ten to fifteen minutes for this exercise. If you only have a few minutes here and there, that's okay—just pause the exercise whenever you need to.

1. Acquire a writing utensil that feels good in your hand.
2. Shake out your body. Stretch your arms, wiggle your toes, and let go of the stories and stresses of the day for a moment. This is a moment for you to listen to *you*.
3. Take three deep breaths. With the first, breathe in, and release. With the second, breathe in, and release with a longer breath out. With the third, take a deep

breath, filling up your body from your toes up to your nose, hold for a moment, and release until your shoulders drop. Repeat that last one if needed.
4. Once your shoulders have dropped, open the worksheet, and look at the prompts.
5. Take a breath (or as long of a break as needed) and then answer each question in its entirety before moving on to the next question.
6. If you notice that your shoulders have crept up, take a moment to pause, shake your body out, and repeat the breathing step from earlier in the exercise.
7. If you hit a question that does not want to be answered, or that you don't have an interest in answering, feel free to skip it. You can either come back to it later, or simply know that you are not called to do it at this time. For some people, this is because your inner Self doesn't want to answer it today, your inner Self is shielding you, the question has no relevance in your current journey, or a few other possible reasons. Don't judge yourself or go digging deeper at this time.
8. Set the worksheet aside. Stand up, stretch out your body, drink some water, or take some other short, non-stressful break.
9. Once you feel refreshed, go back to the first prompt, and read your answers. Do any surprise you? Make you smile? Leave you with something to ponder?
10. Thank yourself for doing the work.

Adaptations

If you have dyslexia, dysgraphia, or a vision impairment, or do not enjoy doing writing-based exercises, you can download the audio file at http://www.passionandsoul.com/beloved.

Once you've downloaded it, you can answer the questions in a few different ways:

A. Write your answers on paper with your chosen writing instrument.
B. Type your answers out on your computer and save them for later.
C. Audio- or video-record your answers on a smartphone, computer, or other device.
D. Answer out loud.
E. Answer in your head.

As with the exercise in the previous chapter, I strongly recommend recording your answers in some way, because the mind can be very good at misremembering or shifting an experience. This does not mean you are evading your own answers. You are experiencing something profoundly human. Recording your answers will also allow you to come back and reflect on them if you repeat the exercise a few hours, days, months, or even years later.

Worksheet

What are eight labels you identify as or with? (For ideas, see the beginning of this chapter.)

"I am…"

1. _____

2. _____

3. _____

4. _____

5. _____

6. _____

7. _____

8. _____

What are four labels others have assigned you?

"Others say I am…"

1. _____

2. _____

3. _____

4. _____

What are eight positive traits you believe that you have?

"I am…"

1. _____

2. _____

3. _____

4. _____

5. _____

6. _____

7. _____

8. _____

What are four positive traits others see in you?

"Others say I am…"

1. _____

2. _____

3. _____

4. _____

What are two labels or identities that are private for you?

"I am…"

1. _____

2. _____

What are four traits you want yourself to improve on?

"I want to be…"

1. _____

2. _____

3. _____

4. _____

What are four actions you can begin to do today to support those improvements?

"I can…"

1. _____

2. _____

3. _____

4. _____

Bonus: Go do the action you said you could begin to do today. When we put off doing things, especially for ourselves, we often start to come up with excuses. We put other projects and other people above ourselves. Listen to you and what *you* want to do. But don't be hard on yourself if you don't take actions right away, or ever do. This work can sometimes take time.

Going Forward

Feel free to return to this exercise at any time, allowing yourself each time to answer without any preconceived judgments or thoughts about how you might have answered previously. As the author, I also give you permission to photocopy or print out these pages for your personal use, so that you can return to the exercise as much as and wherever you like.

Chapter 5

DESERVING DELIGHT: UNDERSTANDING LOVE AND CONNECTION

Love comes in many forms. In the English language, the word "love" becomes cloudy at times, though, confused by the variety of things love can mean in any given situation. When you say "I love you" to another person, what are you trying to communicate to them? That you consider them family? That they are cherished and appreciated? That your romantic heart has their name etched on it? When discussing the ways in which we care for someone, or what sort of relationship we want with them, this lack of words makes it even more challenging to express ourselves.

Communication can break down at many points during any conversation. There are so many steps in the process! First, we think of a concept, and then we turn it into words based on our own understanding of what those words mean to us. Those words then get communicated verbally, on screen, or in other media, before the other person then filters those words through their own life history. Thus, something as supposedly simple as "I love you" can be construed, or misconstrued, in thousands of different ways.

> Love is an action, never simply a *feeling*.
> —BELL HOOKS

SIX FORMS OF LOVE

The Greek language has seven different words for the concept that English bundles into the single word "love": *agape, eros, ludus, philia, philautia, pragma*, and *storge*. In many movies and other media, the concept of *eros* is lifted up as the be-all, end-all—the greatest form of love. It is the madness and passion of "falling in love," by which people fall into an altered state of consciousness under the spell of desire. It is the spark that triggers lips on lips, hips on hips, bodies entwined in a frenzy.

The other form of love that so many celebrate in our culture is *storge*, the love between parents and children. This is held in both the passion parents show in going out of their way to protect their children, as well as in that quietly beating joy or appreciation that healthy and balanced connections have for each other.

In friendships, two different forms of love often come into play. The first is *ludus*, which embodies the emotion of love between children that involves laughter, teasing, and playfulness. Between lovers and adults, this also manifests as giggling, flirting, dancing, and poking fun at one another. The other form of love in friendship is *philia*, a profound loyalty formed at the center of a relationship between two people. This can manifest as a sense of comradery, a willingness to sacrifice deeply for those we care about, or a sincere knowing that these are "our people" that we would do anything for.

Eros, *ludus*, and *philia* can also shape the development of *pragma*, the core sense of understanding that holds strong in long-established couples or connections. *Pragma* is the voice of patience, tolerance, and persistence that allows for an enduring love rather than a fire that burns brightly before flickering out. On the other hand, *agape* is a sort of selfless or holy love that can appear in spiritual connections with divine forces, or people on this plane. In Theravāda Buddhism, the concept of *agape* is similar to *mettā*, or "universal loving kindness," wherein the whole universe, and everything in it, is deserving of this form of love, rather than its belonging to only one thing or person.

These six forms of love are all valuable to consider when we think of ourselves as well. How can your passion bubble up for yourself with *eros*? In what ways does your inner caretaker nurture you with a sense of *storge*? How can you bring joyful, loving fun into your own life with *ludus*, or hold fast for yourself when you need to be protected with a sense of *philia*? Having known yourself your whole life, how can you deeply value and show patience for yourself with *pragma*? How do you deserve *agape*, or allow yourself to connect with divinity or a greater sense of purpose with *agape*?

Together, these concepts also hold space for the seventh form of love, *philautia*. Specifically meant to evoke a sense of self-love, it is a tool that allows us to open a space for us to love others in the world by experiencing self-compassion. This is distinctly different from narcissism, which is an ego-driven or vain admiration for oneself. Named for the Greek god Narcissus, who fell in love with his own reflection, narcissism usually does not leave space for *philautia*. In *philautia*, we see ourselves whole, including the various flaws we have and how we need to learn and grow during life, rather than the myths we might see on the surface of the water that stare back at some clinical narcissists.

In English, though, the word "love" is often a blending of some, many, or all these concepts. It can mean something different each time we use it. And yet, there it is—this word "love" that craves to be expressed.

You deserve that love, or—if that word does not feel like a good fit for you—that care, affection, or attention.

That love is there, in your being, waiting to be expressed by you, for you.

The process of becoming contains a series of undoings. —HG Wyndell

THE FIVE LOVE LANGUAGES

We use many different tools to build various relationships with others. In his book, *The Five Love Languages: The Secret to Love that Lasts*, Gary Chapman puts forth the premise that each of us shows love and affection in different ways and hears it in different ways. As a disclaimer, this concept was built without any studies or proof, from a white, Christian, monogamous lens, and Chapman is not a therapist. That said, this model can be a useful start for looking at how you show care, not just with others—but with yourself.

The forms of expression, or languages, that Chapman presents are:
- Words of affirmation
- Acts of service
- Gifts
- Quality time
- Physical touch

When people begin dating, frequently they do all five. Over time, though, they often revert to one or two that they feel most comfortable (or habitual) expressing. When you are learning how to love yourself, it is important to consider what you, yourself, value. Yes, you can do all five for yourself—and it's wonderful to do so. But what things do you value most as the recipient of your own attention and affection?

WORDS OF AFFIRMATION

If you cherish receiving words of affirmation, finding the perfect song to express the way you feel about your own journey can help you connect deeply with your sense of Self. If a song echoes to your heart about who you are, what would it be like to attend that concert and enjoy it fully? If you don't enjoy the crowds, could you make a space at home to just close your eyes and listen? Another common tool for sharing words of affirmation with ourselves is to take a temporary marker and write positive messages about ourselves in the first person on the mirror to see each morning when we wake up.

Many of us spend time praising others—why shouldn't we tell ourselves what we appreciate about ourselves? Post-it notes on a computer screen or in a notebook that you use for other projects can be great options as well, especially if you share a home with others. If you experience love through words of affirmation but do not write for whatever reason, you can create and listen to your own audio recordings, listen to self-affirmation audio tapes created by others, or watch self-empowerment videos or uplifting movies that remind you of your own strengths. Consider saving quotes that remind you of the things you appreciate about yourself to your desktop or smartphone or finding beautiful artwork that features such words and messages.

Saying "I love you" may seem easiest to "hear" as love, but it is not universally experienced that way. Some people may say that it is easy to say, "I love you," but not show it. Words can be cheap, argues this logic that needs to have "proof" of that thing called love. As a love language, providing acts of service is one such way that we can show love.

> Love without action is meaningless and action without love is irrelevant. —DEEPAK CHOPRA

ACTS OF SERVICE

When doing acts of service for yourself, they can take two major forms: the "little" things and the "big" things. The little things are the day-to-day acts that show that you care, on an ongoing basis. Making the bed for yourself each morning, using your favorite beard conditioner, or taking out the trash are little things you can do for yourself to say that you appreciate yourself. They may not seem like a big deal, but over time, these little acts of service will help you live in a more joyous, present, and self-affirming way. You will be showing yourself that you love *you*, over and over again.

On the other hand, big things include clear statements of self-affection, self-consideration, and self-love. Some people may look at what you consider big things and think that they're not a big deal. For them, cleaning their home may simply be a daily, unconscious task they do. But others find house cleaning a big deal. Choosing to vacuum the house because it needs to be done, and you deserve to live in a house with clean floors, is a loving thing to do for yourself. That is, or can be, a way to say, "I love you."

Whether it is doing repairs around the home, going through the mending, making dinner, washing the car, or clearing out the spam filter on your email, you can give yourself acts of service in a thousand different ways. If you're looking for a job, doing so from a place of consciousness and awareness that you deserve a career that serves your life can be a form of self-love. When doing things for yourself, be aware of any tendency to invoke the word "should"—as in, "I should have done this already"; "This shouldn't be a big deal"; "I shouldn't consider this a form of self-love." Take a deep breath and remember that using "should" is neither kind nor useful. The act is what it is, when it is, and how it is, and it is a form of self-love to and for you.

Erasing "should" from your self-talk is also an act of self-love.

GIFTS

Another way that people show love is through giving and receiving gifts. These can be tokens of affection that tell a person they are being thought of even when the other person isn't around, or deeply considered objects that communicate care. This sort of expression of affection can remind someone that they are loved. Gift giving is not about buying someone something out of obligation though, which can be confusing for those of us growing up in societies where spending money is assumed to be part of various holidays or the only way to show someone we care.

Gifting is not, at its root, about the size or shape of the gift—whether the recipient is someone else or ourselves. Small gifts that do not have to cost money include images cut out from magazines, or images and videos saved from online (such as of cute animals or joyful events). This is the "current you" gifting small things to "future you" to enjoy.

> I grew up believing that gifts were necessary, even if they were last minute, even if they were gifts that the recipients would not like or outright might dislike. Gifts were part of the "last minute Christmas shopping" madness every year.
>
> This led to me hating receiving gifts. What I "heard" from that attempt at love was a sense of obligation or someone brainwashed by culture and upbringing. Then one day, I bought myself a shirt that filled me with joy. Every time I wore it, it lit me up. It was a reminder that I loved myself in getting the shirt, and the message printed on the shirt reminded me of my personal values.
>
> It changed my relationship with giving and receiving gifts. Thoughtfulness—that was the difference. It was not about money, obligation, or specific holidays. It was about thoughtfulness. My thoughtfulness for myself changed the thoughtfulness I brought to gifts I gave to.

Saving trinkets from positive moments with yourself, happy memories that are not necessarily based on others, can be another form of gift giving. Even a pebble from a walk you took can bring back a flood of memories, reminding you of the way you feel about yourself, if it is found and held consciously. Tokens acquired when you're with others can be okay as well, finding those little things for yourself, even when walking a path side by side with another individual. After all, when two people walk side by side, even if they are on the same path, they are still on two different journeys.

Usable gifts can be wonderful as well, because when you use the gift, you can remind yourself that you got it for *you*. New clothes, sports gear, makeup, hunting equipment, and spa products are all examples of tangible, usable gifts. If you're considering giving yourself a more utilitarian and mundane item, such as a washing machine, consider whether it will feel special and self-loving, especially if others will use it or you will use it for others. There are no right answers. In fact, some people find such items especially strong statements of self-love!

QUALITY TIME

You might also be the type of person who experiences love by spending quality time with yourself. Much of chapter 2 expresses just that notion—going out for hikes, seeing movies, or enjoying an extended dinner. Note the word "quality," though. Bring attention to the time you spend with yourself. Five hours of unconscious television time and five minutes of being present while petting your cat often feel different. Finding out which one you prefer is key so that you can give yourself the type of love that serves you.

BECOME YOUR OWN BELOVED

If you crave longer periods of quality time, this can include travel. For some people, travel is about setting out on the open road on their own by loading up the car to drive for three days through small towns, packing up a roller bag to hop a flight to far-off lands, or taking themselves to camp at their favorite birding spot. For extroverts, travel might include going with family, friends, or a tour group. Though this might not sound like self-loving quality time, for an extrovert this might be the perfect way to fuel up those batteries by being present in each of those moments. Intention, and attention, go a long way.

Quality time can fit into smaller windows of time as well. You can listen to an enriching or entertaining podcast in one go or in two-minute bursts in the shower upon returning from work. You can even take walks down memory lane or daydream if you allow yourself to be immersed in those moments.

Repeat After Me:
I deserve love.
I give myself permission
to receive healing love.
I give myself permission
to give healing love.
I give myself permission
to open myself to love.
—LADYSPEECH SANKOFA

PHYSICAL TOUCH

Finally, physical touch is a love language of the skin. It is sinking slowly into a bathtub and feeling your love for yourself as the heat holds your form. It is holding yourself tight on bad days, feeling your own arms wrapped around your body. It is going out for a run, then stopping to feel the breeze against your sweaty brow. It is running your fingers across your braids, bringing awareness to the texture and being profoundly present in the moment. This love language will be explored further in chapter 6 as we dive into the power of senses in relating to ourselves.

A BEAUTIFUL BLEND

Many ways that people show each other love, and that we can show ourselves love, are a blend of these five types of love. Nothing must fall strictly into one category. For example, knitting yourself a sweater combines gift giving, an act of service, and possibly quality time or physical touch depending on the way the yarn feels in your hand. Going to the gym to put in some reps can be a combination of physical touch, acts of service, and quality time. Writing poetry that no one else might ever see could be a tool for words of affirmation, quality time, and even gift giving, if you choose to hang it as a piece of art.

As you build love through these various techniques, you have the opportunity to deepen your connection with yourself. These languages can build a foundation of self-value in life at large or feel like moments of spoiling that only temporarily make you feel good. Neither is better or worse. They are simply tools and opportunities for exploration. How much each language matters to us may shift over time or over different situations, such as who we are with. You may have different desires from one person compared to another, desiring words of affirmation from friends, touch from lovers, and gift receiving from yourself, for example.

THE NEURODIVERGENT LOVE LANGUAGES

Author and activist Amythest Schaber has introduced an alternative concept of love languages. They share experiences of being an autistic, intersex individual with chronic illness with their readers and state that there are five neurodivergent love languages: infodumping, parallel play, support swapping, "Please Crush My Soul Back Into My Body," and penguin pebbling. Though conceptualized as tools useful for individuals on the autism spectrum, I believe they are a useful concept for everyone to consider.

Infodumping is sharing our profound passions with others. This means taking things we have just become passionate about (known as new relationship energy, to be discussed in chapter 9) or lifelong delights and letting another person into the topic they are excited about. By talking for hours or sharing random memes, a person offering infodumping is not being self-centered but instead opening their heart, mind, or spirit. When two people share a common topic for infodumping, it can seem to an outsider like they are obsessive, but instead it is a deep connection between individuals. In self-delight, infodumping can be pursued through pursuing passions, finding peers who have shared interests, creating surroundings that feature your interests, or seeking out spaces where infodumping can take place.

> Passion is energy. Feel the power that comes from focusing on what excites you. —OPRAH WINFREY

In *parallel play*, two or more people share space or time that does not require continuous connection with others. This might include two people reading books in the same room, a group of friends coworking on different projects, or lovers engaging with their own erotic activities side by side. It can also be thought of as spending alone time with another person who also happens to be having alone time or sharing space with another when they need to get something done (also known as "body doubling" in discussions of ADHD). Crafting opportunities for parallel play online or in person becomes an act of self-love, as does attending coworking or other body-doubling spaces, even when you do not know anyone.

Support swapping, also called mutual aid, can take many different forms. For people with chronic illness, one person might bring over food one week while the other person does research into doctors the next. Maybe you like going with your partner to a rally on a topic they are passionate about, but you are not, while later that day they give you a ride to work. Support will look different for each person, and thus what might be a big ask for some people is an easy give for another. This becomes a form of collective care that is incredibly important, especially in the world of disability justice when applied at a group level. Joining such systems becomes an act of self-love, making our caring for others a part of how we care for ourselves.

Though playfully termed, "Please Crush My Soul Back Into My Body" is an important form of care for some individuals. Whether done for themselves or provided by others, deep pressure allows for an outside input that lowers stress. Being held or sharing hugs can also have a calming effect by allowing for a form of coregulation with another individual. As neuroscientist and host of the *Cleaning Up the Mental Mess* podcast Dr. Caroline Leaf describes it, "As you co-regulate with someone, the mirror neurons in their brain are activated, and this enables the person in the deregulated state to literally 'mirror' your calmness." Using weighted blankets, self-bondage, sleep sacks, or a sheet to wrap yourself in is a tool for self-regulation that is a form of self-love.

Finally, *penguin pebbling* is what Amythest Schaber initially refers to as "I found this cool rock/button/leaf/etc. and thought you would like it." It is a way to say that even if someone was not present when an object was obtained, the person who found the object was thinking about them and wanted to share it with the person that was not there. This might just mean, "I saw this rock and thought of you," or it may come with a complete story of how and why the person was in their thoughts. Doing so becomes the act of collecting things that bring ourselves joy. We might use these items (physical or digital) to share stories with others, or as triggers for our own memory to take us back to a moment where we thought of ourselves and thought we would like the thing.

> Raise your awareness and cultivate your uniqueness. —Amit Ray

While the exercise encompasses Chapman's love languages, feel free to reframe the steps using Schaber's neurodivergent love language terms if those serve you better. The exercise can also be expanded to include the "18 Modern Love Languages" model by sexuality educator, relationship coach, and author Anne Hodder-Shipp. Their system approaches the topic outside of Chapman's assumption that monogamous, heterosexual romantic marriage is the only form of healthy relationship, branching out further to include value in many diverse forms of love from a variety of relationships. Applying this work from a self-love lens to hers can be a rich exercise once you have tried this variation.

✧ Exercise: Express Your Love Languages

Knowing that there are many ways to express and receive love, it's important to find out which ones resonate with you the most. Note that how you "hear" love may or may not be identical to how you show love to others or yourself. You may have been taught about love by family members while you were growing up or learned about it by absorbing cultural stories and media. You may also have a habit of expressing love to others in a specific way, but that does not mean it will be how you want to express love to yourself.

Remember as well that love languages, whether presented by Schaber or Chapman, can change over time, or with different people. In this exercise, we are examining how you experience affection today, in this moment. Do not use it as a be-all-end-all answer to how to connect to yourself and others, and certainly do not consider it a way to keep score as to who in your life may be trying to show you love or not.

If you're listening to this in audiobook form, you can download the written worksheet at http://www.passionandsoul.com/beloved.

Remember: with each of the exercises in this book, you get to choose if and how to engage with them. The choice is always yours.

1. Write down each of the five love languages on a page of paper or use the worksheet. If Schaber's system appeals to you more, cross out Chapman's system and replace the languages shown on the worksheet.
2. Go back through this chapter and use the examples provided as a starting point to brainstorm a few ideas for each of these techniques for expressing love, affection, and appreciation to yourself. Then write down two to four ideas for each love language of things you might enjoy receiving from yourself or giving to yourself.
3. Set down the list for five to ten minutes and come back to look at it with fresh eyes.

4. Put a star next to one activity from each love language category that you can commit to doing in the next week.
5. Remember to set yourself up for success—promising yourself to go climb a mountain, if you know you have a six-day workweek and live in the city, might not be feasible, but committing to take a five-minute walk might be something you can follow through on. This is not a competition.
6. Write down each of the things you will do in the next week, noting any modifications made to set yourself up for success.
7. Over the course of the week, make a commitment to show yourself love in these five ways. Some people may find it useful to choose one to do each day, make a list of all five and check them off as they go, or use some other tool to remind themselves.
8. No matter how the week goes, remember to thank yourself for doing the work.

Adaptations

If you have dyslexia, dysgraphia, or a vision impairment, or do not enjoy doing writing-based exercises, you can download the audio file for the worksheet at http://www.passionandsoul.com/beloved.

Once you've downloaded it, you can answer the questions in a few different ways:

A. Write your answers on paper with your chosen writing instrument.
B. Type your answers out on your computer and save your answers for later.
C. Audio- or video-record your answers on a smartphone, computer, or other device.
D. Answer out loud.
E. Answer in your head.

As with the previous exercises, I strongly recommend recording your answers in some way, because the mind can be very good at misremembering or shifting an experience. This does not mean you are evading your own answers. You are experiencing something profoundly human. Recording your answers will also allow you to come back and reflect on them if you repeat the exercise a few hours, days, months, or even years later.

Worksheet

Words of Affirmation

1. _____

2. _____

3. _____

4. _____

Acts of Service

1. _____

2. _____

3. _____

4. _____

Gifts

1. _____

2. _____

3. _____

4. _____

Quality Time

1. _____

2. _____

3. _____

4. _____

Physical Touch

1. _____

2. _____

3. _____

4. _____

Going Forward

After a week, come back to the worksheet or reflect upon what the experience was like for you. Were there types of receiving that felt more like love to you? What type of love?

If, at the end of the week, you were not able to do all five expressions of the love languages, be gentle. Do not use the word "should." This is not a competition, and there is nothing wrong with having prioritized other things during the week of this exercise.

Take a chance instead to reflect on the week and see if you did anything to show yourself love, appreciation, or care. Did you straighten your desk out at the end of the day, giving yourself a peaceful workplace to return to the next day? Make yourself a meal or snack that you enjoyed? Patted yourself on your own back for having worked on something difficult? Taken a moment under the shower to feel the water wash over you? Listened to the lyrics of a song and tuned the rest of the world out for a moment? These seemingly little things are also expressions of love and care and are ways you may have been communicating to yourself, even in a hectic period, that you matter to you.

Remember that showing yourself love is not a one-and-done deal. Feel free to revisit your lists often, revise them as you like, and practice as many of the items as you desire on an ongoing basis. As the author, I also give you permission to photocopy or print out these pages for your personal use, so that you can return to your lists as much as and wherever you like.

Chapter 6

DANCING WITH YOURSELF: EXPLORING SENSUALITY

Taste. Smell. Sight. Sound. Touch. Our senses are our gateway to the world, and our gateway to ourselves as well. It is a myth that we interact with ourselves only in our own head. We interact with ourselves and the world through all our senses and more.

I was introduced to the notion of taste being an act of self-love by a friend of mine who was a dance partner of mine. They had brought fresh mangoes with them to one dance, and at the end of the night, they said that they were going to go enjoy their mango with themself. It wasn't that my dance partner wanted to be away from me; it's that they really wanted to be with themself and that mango.

I slowly cut the mango open. The juice began dripping down my fingers as the flesh gave way. I lifted the first piece and placed it between my lips, letting the tender fruit fill my mouth. As I closed my eyes, in that moment, I and the mango were all that existed in the world.

This was a form of what gets called mindfulness. Mindfulness is a state of being where a person focuses their attention on the present moment. It is done not by dissociating from what else is happening around us, but by acknowledging our thoughts, feelings, and sensations, and then letting go of what is extraneous to that which an individual is being mindful of.

Plant your own garden and decorate your own soul, instead of waiting for someone to bring you flowers. —Jorge Luis Borges

In the case of eating the mango, the action was not just about eating the mango. It was about being present with that mango, and even more so, being present with myself. How did that mango taste? What did it feel like on my fingers? How was I, then and there, in that moment? I was not thinking of how I "should" feel or what it "should" taste like. I did not use future-speak ("How will this taste?") or past-speak ("This is how it tasted."). Instead, I was there, in the moment, experiencing the mango.

We have a variety of opportunities to practice mindfulness, from dancing when no one is watching to going to a massage therapist. Our culture tells us a story of what mindfulness should look like. Buddhist monks in robes. Yoga studios. But it can be just as accessible when throwing a basketball, feeling the bumps of the rubber under your fingertips and concrete under your feet, or making a quilt, feeling the fabric slide by as you sew.

Ask yourself—how do you get into your body? Your body is just as important a part of you as your mind is.

THE HEDONISM TRAP

Another form of being present is hedonism. This term denotes the pursuit of pleasure and engaging deeply in sensual indulgence. As mindfulness focuses on noting and letting go of extraneous information, hedonism embraces all the sensations present and encourages the person being hedonistic to override those extraneous thoughts with the pleasure present in the experience. In the case of the mango, mindfulness was my tasting the mango juice running down and being present with it, whereas hedonism might have involved moaning as I experienced the best mango I could have in that moment.

Hedonism becomes problematic when the pursuit of pleasure overrides the possibilities of living a complex life. Check whether you are using an experience as a chance to dive into life and be present, or to flee from life—as an escape from what is happening in the world around you. Being so present in each moment that you do not plan for the future or reflect upon the past to learn from it can be harmful. However, hedonism and mindfulness can both be positive tools if we actively and consciously incorporate our full selves into our lives as a whole.

SAVOR YOUR SENSES

You can experiment with your senses right now! As you read this book, feel the pages under your fingertips or the surface of your e-book reader in your hands. If you're listening to the audio version, feel the texture of your clothing or skin. Notice your body posture and adjust yourself in a way that cares for this amazing body that you live in. Roll back your shoulders and keep reading or listening. Notice how your physical experience is affecting your emotions, how your emotions are affecting the words you perceive, and how these words may be affecting your body in turn. Is your heart rate going up, or are you breathing more slowly than you were before?

Even when we are with other people, we can take a moment to be in our bodies and present with ourselves. If you are kayaking with a friend, take a deep breath and smell the air. Look around and be awed by the natural beauty around you. If you are listening to an album with a lover, close your eyes for a moment to listen to each instrument, acknowledge the lyrics, and feel the way your flesh responds to the melody.

It is not necessary to share these moments with someone else to have them be valuable, despite what culture tells us. In some cases, it's not even possible. The person next to us cannot have the exact experience we are having, because they are in *their* body.

Different individuals will filter their experiences through their own history, their own perspective, and their own flesh. I was hiking side by side with my lover one day. We both had our cameras with us and were snapping images to enjoy later. At the end of the hike, we went home, downloaded the pictures, and shared them with each other.

No two images were the same. I had shot photos of the trees, the sky, and the shadows cast as the sun moved across the sky. My lover had mostly taken pictures of the creatures that passed by, including me and a guy with a lizard on his head. At first, I wanted to ask my lover why they took the pictures that they did, why their lens of reality was so different. I even judged them a bit, wondering why they had not seen the raw plant-based beauty I had. Then I judged myself for not taking more pictures of them or of animals.

Then it struck me. Neither of our approaches was better or worse. Both of us were simply experiencing the world filtered through our own senses and internal lenses. This was a beautiful thing.

THE POWER OF CLOTHING

Every day, we can experience our senses through the act of getting dressed. Each time we don clothing, we are painting a story for the world and for ourselves. Uniforms don't paint us as individuals; they show the outside world how to treat us and let us know who our peers are on our path. Putting on blue jeans and a tee shirt crafts a different story for others who encounter us than putting on a power suit or overalls.

What we wear also affects how we see ourselves. For those in military service, wearing fatigues, donning a dress uniform or being out of uniform can hack one's mind when looking in a mirror. This is the sense of sight hard at play affecting your sense of identity through the cut and type of costume you wear. As legendary drag performer RuPaul has said, "We're all born naked, and the rest is drag." Any sort of clothing can help us transform or can transform us—if we become conscious of it.

How do you want to dress for yourself? If you are staying at home for the day, what would feel good to you? Going to the office or spending time with family may constrict those choices, but many of us do not take the time to ask ourselves what would excite us and our senses. Would exciting clothing for you be based on color? Texture? Cultural aesthetic? Perhaps you long to wear purple or light blue. Perhaps silks or heavy canvas. Perhaps you are haute couture or enjoy flannel and cargo pants.

Cultures and subcultures state what a person should wear. Nationality, religion, gender, and more affect our clothing choices. How many men might enjoy the easy comfort of flowing skirts if our choices were just about the joy of such a garment rather than the story our culture tells us about what wearing that skirt "means?" What would the world look like if children could wear whatever makes them smile or whatever feels good on their skin?

Practicing self-love means taking the opportunity to pause and consider why you are wearing what you wear. Ask yourself what might happen if you wore what you—yourself, your Self—wanted to wear.

Your mood can also be affected by what you choose to wear. For many people seeking to enjoy an erotic experience, putting on sexy underpants, high heels, flowing robes, tight leather, or a specific scent can help ignite their passion. Dressing for decadence can also elicit these feelings in others, but when you are working on your relationship with yourself, look at what works for *you*. Instead of asking a partner what turns them on, ask yourself what turns you on. Is it smelling incense or letting a log fire burn? Perhaps it is lowering the lights or laying rope and chain down on the bed. Maybe it is walking outside on a sunny day or listening to an R&B album you love.

> To love oneself is the beginning of a lifelong romance. —OSCAR WILDE

SEXUAL AND SENSUAL AUTHENTICITY

Embracing our senses can also include diving into our sexual connections with ourselves. What does your body long for? Using mindfulness techniques, we can note the sensations we experience as our hands glide across our body, being fully present in the moment. Enjoying hedonism, we can experience the depth of an experience and allow ourselves to be lost in the decadence. Culture often tells us what our bodies should experience or desire, tells us what should turn us on, tells us that if we fall outside the societal stories presented by our schools, parents, religion, or pornography that we and our experiences are not "appropriate."

What does your erotic authenticity look like? What does your sensual authenticity look like? Instead of separating your diverse erotic sensual experiences, consider that all of them are about embracing your senses. These experiences are then filtered through their own senses and internal filters. No filters are better or worse; they simply are different for different people.

Oftentimes, we save these questions of what we are "into" for special encounters with a beloved, but as you're learning, you can be your own beloved. You deserve the opportunity to explore your passions and desires. This is true whether the experience involves an autoerotic encounter, a mug of hot cocoa, or a calming sound. Being sexual is no better than being asexual; it is simply a different way we engage with our senses and our desires. You deserve to tap into your erotic Self.

As Audre Lorde states in *Uses of the Erotic: The Erotic as Power*, "The erotic is a measure between the beginnings of our sense of self and the chaos of our strongest feelings. It is an internal sense of satisfaction to which, once we have experienced it, we know we can aspire. For having experienced the fullness of this depth of feeling and recognizing its power, in honor and self-respect we can require no less of ourselves." Thus, the concept of the erotic is also far deeper than the exploration of the sensual and, if it is removed from a lens of consumerist debauchery, can help us find more meaning in life at large.

Consider taking a long bath with yourself, soaking in still water, or laughing in a tub full of bubbles. Maybe you would enjoy spending time in the shower, letting the stream rush over your face and down your shoulders while the hot water mists up around you. Perhaps you would relish brushing your hair as you close your eyes, feeling each stroke across your scalp. You might even enjoy slapping leather across various parts of your body, leaving welts upon your own flesh, feeling the heat of each one afterwards.

Engaging the senses also applies to what our eyes take in. We absorb the visual world around us, and this absorption helps paint a story of how we feel and what we think, in turn affecting how we walk through the world. If you are crafting a world for yourself where you thrive, what will you surround yourself with? People moving in together often think about this. Whose paintings will go up on the walls? Which taxidermy or sculpture will express each person's personality? These questions arise whether those other people are our children, parents, romantic partners, roommates, or platonic life-mates.

Beauty begins the moment you decide to be yourself. —Coco Chanel

If you are living on your own, ask yourself the same questions. How can you express your personality and affirm your sense of Self with the world around you? This process becomes a loop—you affect the world around you, and the world you have crafted affects you in turn. Have you hung that piece of art every single time you've moved somewhere new because it brings you joy and positive memories, or is it hanging there out of a sense of obligation or resentment? There is nothing wrong with choosing to have an item in your environment because you feel like you owe it to someone—but make sure you do so consciously and that its presence is not pulling you down. Consider not only what will help you survive, but what around you might help you thrive or delight on your journey.

Do you live with others? What small objects can you sprinkle around that claim your space as being yours or supportive of you? For some, this might mean building a small altar or hiding small objects that symbolically enforce self-identity. Others might value intentionally sitting down with the other individuals they live with and making sure that all parties play an active part in codesigning the home from the ground on up.

CURATE YOUR DIGITAL HOME

Transient individuals, people who spend a lot of time on the road, or people who have little say in what their immediate surroundings look like can travel with a small object they can use as a touchstone or make active choices about what they take in digitally. Building folders full of images, photos you took or downloaded, can be a chance during the day to stop and absorb beauty or inspiration. Social media feeds that are likely to offer aesthetic inspiration can also be useful, but keep in mind that some social media also carries stressful topics that can affect your sense of well-being.

Choosing which social media groups and individuals you follow online is a form of curating your own digital home. Many people believe it's important to be a part of the political and social dialogue, but you get to determine how people interact on your personal web platforms, if you choose to use them at all. You get to choose to not follow people, even family and close friends, who disrespect you and spread hateful language. Doing so can be an act of self-love. For many people of color, LGBTQ+ individuals, people with disabilities, and folks with a variety of nationality backgrounds or religious beliefs, the political is inherently personal after all.

> May the stars carry your sadness away,
> May the flowers fill your heart with beauty,
> May hope forever wipe away your tears.
> And, above all, may silence make you strong.
> —Chief Dan George

GIVE YOURSELF A BREAK

Stepping away from the internet or closing your eyes at your desk can allow you to tap back into your senses. What is the temperature of the room? How is your spine aligned? What else is in your space? How does the room smell? What sounds are you listening to? When is the last time you stepped away from that screen?

Your senses are a powerful tool that you can use to get to know yourself, not just to know a moment. When you're stressed, how does your body hold that stress? What senses do you focus or fixate on? What senses do you tend to block out? As you learn about your senses and indulge in them, you develop self-awareness. Giving yourself a break, or diving fully into those senses, becomes a gift to yourself. You deserve to know yourself better, and to embrace your authentic Self as your own beloved.

✧ Exercise A: Dive into Your Senses

Stopping to smell the roses has power.

What does your partner, yourself, notice when you take in a moment? How can you experience a moment fully?

In this exercise, we will start by diving into our senses and being present with our body and emotions. To do so, we will begin with a series of exercises in mindfulness and hedonism alike. This will require three to ten minutes of time when you are not doing any other activities—though, if interrupted, you can return to the exercise.

If you do not have a specific sense or senses, such as sight or sound, available to you, tap into the sense(s) you do have and skip over questions that do not apply. Audio and written versions of these questions are also available on my website at http://www.passionandsoul.com/beloved.

Remember: with each of the exercises in this book, you get to choose if and how to engage with them. The choice is always yours.

1. Pour or open a beverage of your choice.
2. Drink a few sips and answer the following questions:
    a. What does your drink look like?
    b. How does it taste?
    c. What does it smell like?
    d. What is its temperature?
3. Then expand your senses by answering:
    e. What does your glass, can, bottle, or mug look like?
    f. What texture is the container the beverage is in?
    g. What does tapping your fingers or nails on the container sound like?
4. Having become aware of your drink, consider your own body:
    h. How is your body posed right now? Are you hunched over or sitting up straight?
    i. Where is your body carrying stress or tension?
    j. Has drinking this beverage changed your body position or body stress?
5. Roll your shoulders back, put the drink under your nose, and take a deep breath. Smell the drink. Release your breath. Take a second deep breath while smelling the drink. Release again, relaxing your shoulders and jaw, then answer:
    k. Has this changed how your body is positioned?
    l. How has your mood changed?
    m. Have you noticed anything new about your body or your beverage?

6. Close your eyes and let the beverage permeate your senses. Take a sip and feel the temperature on your tongue and under the pads of your fingers. Let the taste fill your mouth. For a moment, let the drink be all that exists in your world.
7. Emote the emotions that come up for you. A slight grin, a large smile, a small "yum," or a dramatic moan are examples of emoting emotions. If the feelings that arise are not positive ones, give yourself permission to frown, sigh, or even set down your beverage and discontinue this exercise. Every emotion is perfectly acceptable.
8. Finish your drink at your own pace. Note any differences in your body between when you began the exercise and when you finished. Feel free to repeat this exercise any time you like.
9. Thank yourself for doing the work.

✧ Exercise B: Go on a Sensuality Date

What would it look like for you to embrace your senses for a date with yourself? Look at your date from chapter 2 and consider using this as an exercise for that second date you promised yourself if you haven't had that date already.

As with the date you had before, this does not have to take an entire evening. Remember that the time you take (or do not take) for yourself might be communication to your inner Self about how you value yourself. This is a chance to spoil yourself or simply enjoy the fullness of being present with yourself.

Remember: with each of the exercises in this book, you get to choose if and how to engage with them. The choice is always yours.

1. Decide on where to go for your date and what you will get up to. Will you be going for a long run with yourself or making a simple meal at home? Does a sexual evening with yourself or a quiet morning reading a book call to you? Perhaps you would love the chance to go rock climbing or have a night on the town attending the theater and enjoying dessert.
2. Get dressed for your date. How we are "supposed" to dress for a date is often dictated by our culture's assumptions of what is appropriate. You might have even dressed "appropriately" for your first date with yourself. If you are dressing for you, though, what feels good? Run your hands over your wardrobe items and see which shirts, trousers, dresses, or underwear feel best under your fingers. If you were to choose based entirely on texture, what would you choose? What colors are calling to you? Perhaps the blue of that top you rarely wear? Perhaps your story of a date involves wearing a suit, but you want to wear your old flannel shirt? Dress for you!
3. Do you want to wear a fragrance? Choose specific jewelry? Wear a specific type of footwear? Complete your look/scent for your date.
4. Take a moment to tune into your senses and notice what your outfit brings up for you emotionally as well. Are you more playful because of a specific wardrobe

item—or a bit nervous, or more self-confident? If you are experiencing uncertainty about wearing your outfit in the world at large, make sure to care for yourself, your safety, and your complex layers of identity. There is nothing wrong with changing clothes. Consider dressing to your delight even for just five minutes a chance to explore your senses and desires.

5. Head off to your date!
6. During your date, stop from time to time and touch base with your senses. Taste. Smell. Sight. Sound. Touch. You might also have a sense that encompasses something beyond these experiences. If you're on a run, note what your skin feels like as you sprint, as well as when you pause to have a drink of water. If you're having a meal at home, what do your spices taste like before and after you cook them? If you're having a sexually or sensually intimate encounter, as your fingers dance over your skin, listen to the sounds of your own breath as your excitement builds. If you're reading a book, when turning the pages under your fingers, note the quality of the light in the room and lift the book to breathe in the scent of the tome itself.
7. After your date, remember that your senses don't end there. Continue your awareness throughout the day or night. Remember that if your senses drift away and you go on "autopilot," you can always come back to the here and now. If your senses overwhelm you, you can take a deep breath and release, letting go of the stress that your hyperawareness has built.
8. Thank yourself for going on the date with yourself.

Going Forward

Regularly making time for one or both exercises can be a wonderful exploration of and gift to yourself, as well as a gateway to deepening your self-connection and self-knowledge. Perhaps you'll replace the beverage in Exercise A with a chocolate truffle or piece of fruit. Perhaps what you choose to wear on your date for Exercise B, or where you go and what you do, will change over time. No matter how these exercises evolve for you, be open to and celebrate the evolution.

Chapter 7

I ME WED: MAKING COMMITMENTS

Most of us are aware of the commitments we make to others.

The commitments we make can vary widely. One might agree to pay rent on the first of each month or pledge to take out the trash. We might tell a coworker that we will get a report to them by the next day or promise a friend to take care of their child if the friend ever passes away.

Some of these commitments might feel bigger or smaller than others, but that is based entirely on the experience of the person making the commitment. For some people, paying the rent might be no big deal, while for others who are balancing three jobs and medical bills, it is an ordeal every time. Taking out the trash might be a simple, even unconscious, exercise for some, while those living with physical disabilities may need to coordinate several factors to make that seemingly "simple" promise come to pass. Unless we are in someone else's skin, we don't know whether the thing they are agreeing to is a "big deal" or not.

> Next time you feel agitated because you are falling back into past patterns, remember that simply being aware that you have fallen back into repeating the past is a sign of progress. Self-awareness comes before the great leap forward in your personal transformation. —YUNG PUEBLO

WHAT COMMITMENTS HAVE YOU MADE?

Perhaps the commitments listed above were not even made for the benefit of the person on the receiving end. Are you agreeing to get in that report because your coworker has asked you to, or even wants you to? Or are you saying you will get the report in because you thrive under a deadline and with someone holding you responsible? Learning for yourself which you are can help tease out why you are agreeing to something. If the person you are promising something to couldn't care less about it, that does not make it an invalid promise. It makes it a promise to yourself.

Have you made commitments to yourself in the past? Most of us have, but perhaps not always consciously. Have you followed through on these commitments, or are you more likely to keep your word to other people than to yourself?

If you don't follow through with others but do with yourself, is there a reason? If you follow through with others but don't with yourself, why is that? This may seem like a question about what keeps us from following through on what we say we will do, but it is also a question of why we make promises to do things that some part of us cannot, will not, or are not sure we will be able to do.

> I am a deeply spiritual person. Along my spiritual path, I've had a variety of times when I made promises to myself that I would adhere to certain daily practices or activities. Most of the time, I did not keep these commitments.
>
> One day, I realized I was not setting myself up for success. I had a belief that if I was not perfect, I had to set my commitment aside. That I had failed. I was allowing "should" thoughts to affect me.
>
> I believed I had to make all-or-nothing commitments. These are important for some spiritual or religious practices, but not for the ones I was making. Becoming aware of how my brain worked around returning to daily spiritual practices even after a time of not doing them helped me make better promises to myself in other parts of my life. Some of us thrive in all or nothing and others thrive in ebb and flow. My brain is unique, and so is yours.

MARRIAGE AND LEGAL VOWS

In the world of romantic connection in the American culture and many other cultures, one of the most iconic forms of commitment is that of the marriage vow. Historically, the marriage vow was a legal contract. It ranged from being a simple agreement between two families to being an ornate legal document that listed property rights. Some vows and legal agreements adhere to laws of the land, while others, such as the signing of a *ketubah* (marriage contract) in Jewish weddings, follow specific religious laws and traditions.

In modern times, the world of romance has blended with legal agreements and spiritual commitments. Many people marry without it being about bringing together two families, forming political alliances, or pre-planning for child-rearing. They may not even have sat with why they are saying the vows that will pass from their lips or check with themselves that specific vows are what they want to agree to.

Beyond the legal connotations, though, marriage has specific meaning to each of us. We can picture what the words "I'm married" mean. Walking side by side. Love. Romance. Meaningful connection. Building a life together. Something else entirely?

What does marriage, or a relationship commitment, mean to you?

I started to ask myself that very question and went on a quest into it. I journaled, talked to close friends, read books on relationships, and meditated on the topic. I spoke with folks about their relationships with themselves and what that looked like for them. Along the way, it became a question of what vows I would make to myself if I were to commit to myself. This would apply whether my vows were about being my own partner or other people's partner. Why was I thinking of making certain vows and not others?

This question became the starting point for a much broader topic. It was a tool to help me acknowledge that I was with me for life. I came to realize that others might come and go, but I am here for me. Even if others are here too, I must be happy, whole, and bonded with me. I realized that the idea of a union enforced that concept. Based on my self-exploration, I desired to get married to myself.

Connecting with ourselves is like connecting in any relationship. Sometimes love happens and no commitment ceremony is desired at all. Being together is perfect, with no pomp or circumstance needed. For others, a marriage means something else. Each person or group we connect to will think of different meanings or images when they consider the notions of commitment and sharing out loud what those things look like for us is important.

THE MANY KINDS OF "SHIPS"

So many relationship types exist. Friend. Ally. Sibling. Co-adventurer. Our culture may paint a story that these are not as lauded as a marriage, but how many of us have a friendship that will be with us until the end of our lives, while romantic or sexual relationships may come and go? Our commitments to our friends are just as important, and becoming our own friends might be, for some people, even more powerful.

BECOME YOUR OWN BELOVED

We have so many "ships" to choose from! Friendships, partnerships, mentorships...what kind of "ship" do you want on your journey with yourself? If we imagine relationships as literal ships, there are no bad types of ships. There are simply ships that do not serve our needs, wants, desires, goals, plans, passions, hopes, and dreams. If I long for a decadent gondola ride, lying back and taking in every view as another pushes my way, I may be deeply upset to find myself aboard a minesweeper pushing its way through enemy territory. This does not make the minesweeper in service to the Navy a bad ship. It only makes it not a gondola.

Some of us want to know what kind of vessel we are boarding when we start building a connection with ourselves, but don't need to know where it is going. Others care more about the destination, but the ship will reveal itself over time. Perhaps you know how to build certain types of relationships but not others. If you know how to build a friendship, for example, building a friendship with yourself might be simpler than building another type of relationship with yourself. The shape of your "ship," along with your desired destination with yourself, will affect the types of commitment you make to you.

It's hard to be proud of yourself when you don't have a big support system cheering you on. But your accomplishments are still worth celebrating. —Dominee Calderon

COMMITMENT TOKENS

When people make commitments to each other, it's not uncommon to exchange tokens that remind those wearing them, and those around them, of the promises they have made. A ring on a finger, or a necklace with half a heart hanging from it, can remind each party of the other person and that person's importance. Matching tattoos or piercings can do the same thing in a form that cannot easily be removed. For some people, never taking off a ring makes the commitment stronger, while others might be deeply reminded of their commitment by taking the ring off each night and putting it back on each morning.

Not every relationship needs a token that's wearable. It might be a piece of artwork that hangs on the wall. It might be putting someone on a list of friends you'll see updates from on social media. It might be listening to the music mix they gave you when you're feeling lonely.

If you were to get a token for yourself, what would it be? Would it be a ring you would wear every day, or the tattoo you've always wanted? Might you create a playlist of your favorite music to enjoy, or invest in a cologne that makes you happy when you wear it? Perhaps you would get a quality pair of shoes that helps you consider your next steps forward, or a necklace that you put on when you want to be reminded of your values or desired direction in life.

Whether you choose to use tokens or not, you can use commitments in many ways to evolve a relationship. Some people might be on a "relationship escalator" with a partner that includes dating first, proposing to them, having a wedding, and then being married. They might go in a different order in some cultures, with families and matchmakers connecting a couple, a proposal taking place, then a wedding occurring, before the couple gets to know each other better by building love over time.

In connecting with yourself, you might make a commitment to yourself and then build a deeper bond, or you might connect with yourself deeply before making a commitment. Choose the route that is right for you.

CHOOSING COMMITMENT TYPES

When someone gets engaged, it is often because one partner has taken initiative. An engagement also can be pre-discussed, with each person having an equal say in the decision or can be a grand production involving friends and family and using dramatic acts of affection.

Marriage ceremonies can be just as varied. Some are small affairs that only involve close friends or an elopement to Las Vegas. Others might involve hundreds of witnesses at a sacred place, or years of planning the perfect getaway experience.

There is no right way to solidify a commitment, whether it is with others or with yourself. Perhaps you could whisper privately to yourself in the middle of the night or have an impressive affair with cake and all. You might want to tell a few folks in advance so they can celebrate with you, or a group of people all could bring mirrors and commit to their own selves at the same time. Sit with yourself and consider what matters to you while making such decisions. If having witnesses present matters, be honest with yourself about that, just as much as if you want to keep this as something private for only you.

Vows can be powerful for many people. As you will be living with yourself for the rest of your life, no matter who else you might be in relationship with, what sort of oath would be meaningful to you, from you? This can take the form of marriage, but it would be just as powerful to make a deep friendship commitment to yourself. Whatever term or structure you use to identify your internal relationship, your commitment to yourself has the power to move you forward in life.

> Loving yourself...does not mean being self-absorbed or narcissistic, or disregarding others. Rather it means welcoming yourself as the most honored guest in your own heart, a guest worthy of respect, a lovable companion.
> —Margot Anand

Though we can make vows to ourselves in any form, drawing upon terms like spouse, life-mate, partner, wife, and husband can evoke certain images and archetypes in our subconscious mind. Be forewarned, the subconscious mind can also pull up stories of such relationships from the past. If your parents had a nasty divorce or held violence in their relationship, or if you once had a spouse who embedded negative meaning into the terms mentioned, you can carry that association forward with these terms as well. Consider choosing terms that support you by either reclaiming those terms, processing past traumas, or using terms with no associated toxicity.

If you were to get married to yourself, how would you hold yourself to those vows? After all, we are each walking with ourselves for life. There are no easy divorce options, as it were, though transforming the relationship might be an option. Think about this as you consider the types of vows you want to make to yourself. This is not about cookie-cutter vows others take—it is about something meaningful to you.

✧ EXERCISE: WRITE YOUR VOWS

No matter what kind of relationship you have or are forming with yourself, you can make commitments to yourself. These can be as big or small as you are moved to make, knowing that what is big or small is entirely subjective.

New to this concept or not feeling ready to make a big leap? Consider starting small and working up. Remember that this exercise is simply about writing a vow; you don't have to commit to the vow right now or ever. Consider this a chance to brainstorm what matters to you.

If you're listening to this in audiobook form, you can download a written version of these steps at http://www.passionandsoul.com/beloved.

Remember: with each of the exercises in this book, you get to choose if and how to engage with them. The choice is always yours.

1. Set aside five to ten minutes for the first segment of this exercise.
2. Acquire a writing utensil that feels good in your hand.

3. Shake out your body. Stretch your arms, wiggle your toes, and let go of the stories and stresses of the day for a moment. This is a moment for you to listen to *you*.
4. Take three deep breaths. With the first, breathe in, and release. With the second, breathe in, and release with a longer breath out. With the third, take a deep breath, filling up your body from your toes up to your nose, hold for a moment, and release until your shoulders drop. Repeat that last one if needed.
5. Come up with one way you can commit to yourself *right now* that feels small to you, short term. Write it down here:

_____

_____

6. If you have decided to continue by following through with this commitment, touch base with yourself a few days later about it. Look at what you wrote down. How have you been doing with this commitment? How does it feel for you?
7. A few weeks later, check in again. Go ahead and put it in your calendar to remember to do so—some of us thrive using such tools. How is it going?
8. Recommit if desired. What has helped you follow through on the commitment? Internal desires, daily reminders, external support, scheduling, self-prizes,

inspiration, good feelings, or something else entirely. Write some of those answers down here::

_____

_____

9. If you had chosen to follow through on the commitment but then didn't, examine why. Write down some of the answers you come up with here:

_____

_____

10. Thank yourself for doing the work.

Adaptations

If you have dyslexia, dysgraphia, or a vision impairment, or do not enjoy doing writing-based exercises, you can download the audio file for the worksheet at http://www.passionandsoul.com/beloved.

Once you've downloaded it, you can answer the questions in a few different ways:

A. Write your answers on paper with your chosen writing instrument.

B. Type your answers out on your computer and save them for later.
C. Audio- or video-record your answers on a smartphone, computer, or other device.
D. Answer out loud.
E. Answer in your head.

As with the previous exercises, I strongly recommend recording your commitment in some way, so you can come back to it later instead of relying on memory.

Going Forward

Your commitments might evolve over time. Consider revisiting them after a month or two, or longer. You can make a new commitment or revise the same commitment knowing that you're approaching it from a different mindset. If the first time around was a good fit for you, consider trying for something that feels bigger, with the information you've gained, or for a second, smaller commitment. Write your new or repeated commitment here (or type, audio-record, or video-record it):

_____

_____

And remember to thank yourself for doing the work!

Chapter 8

PLEASE FORGIVE ME: MOVING PAST THE PAST

Content warning: *Discussions of self-injury and abusive behavior.*

We all experience bumps, turbulence, disappointments, and even heartbreak.

Most of us have disappointed ourselves at one point or another. We didn't take out the trash and now the house smells. We ate an entire cake instead of one slice, and now we feel sick or concerned about our health. We let a toxic person back into our lives.

When disappointment comes from an outside source, we can examine it more easily. If someone didn't take out the trash, we can look at the issue from a distance, because it's about someone else. The person didn't take out the trash. From this vantage point, we can name our emotions: "I am sad"; "I am disappointed"; "I am angry." Perhaps we list the possible reasons the person didn't take out the trash or prepare to have a discussion with them about it. We might devise a plan: to ask them again; to take out the trash ourselves; to ask them to handle another task; to chastise them or maybe ground them. We might get frustrated with ourselves for asking them in the first place. We might even lash out with words or actions.

Life is too short to spend another day at war with yourself. —Ritu Ghatourey

NEGATIVE SELF-PERCEPTION AS SELF-INJURY

We can respond in a thousand different ways, whether the issue is with someone else or with ourselves. When we disappoint ourselves, though, it can be hard to respond objectively because there is no space between the action of the issue (taking out the trash in this case) and the person with whom that action is associated (us). We might even add extra layers or meaning to the situation rather than simply naming the action: "I'm frustrated that I did not take out the trash" becomes "I'm frustrated at myself for not doing something yet again—I am such a failure." We jump from noting the emotion to engaging in negative self-perception. However, doing so is a form of self-injurious behavior.

When most people think of self-injury, they think of people cutting themselves or doing drugs. In many cases, these actions are tools to feel something else other than the emotional pain of inner turmoil. For the person harming themself, these actions hurt less than the pain of the internal dialogue or external situation. The actions allow the person to disassociate from what is happening inside their head or in the world around them, or to be distracted for a period.

Self-injury can take many forms, though—forms that if we saw someone we care about experiencing, we might discuss it with them. Abuse can be verbal, physical, psychological, emotional, spiritual, or sexual. But what happens when that abusive behavior is coming from ourselves?

Many of us say profoundly cruel things to ourselves, things that we would never allow another person to say to us or someone we care about. We also might deny ourselves pleasure, overwork past the point of exhaustion, or put ourselves in toxic situations. Whether punishing our bodies or bruising our hearts, we can be our own abusive partners.

If you do this to yourself, what are you getting out of it? There is always some kind of benefit, as paradoxical as it may sound, because otherwise you wouldn't do it. In the case of yelling at yourself, for example, do you get a sense of comfort because others have said those words to you in the past, and that pain is wrapped around your perception of love? Do you get a moment of relief from taking it out on yourself rather than accidentally hurting someone else? Do you get a chance to externalize the emotion so that your internal dialogue can stand up for you, making it so you can be your own hero or rescuer? Examining your "whys" allows you to start teasing apart where this negative talk or behavior is coming from.

Your sadness doesn't make you less of a human being. In fact, it makes you more. More expansive. More connected. Painfully beautiful. Raw. Open. Completely alive. —Panache Desai

REPERCUSSIONS AND SHIFTING CONSCIOUSNESS

Sometimes, though, the pain comes not from a self-abusive response but rather simply from not having done something we meant to do. Just as we might come up with reasons another person didn't take out the trash, which can help us feel better about it, we might do the same with ourselves. It's important to understand the difference between reasons and excuses. "Reason implies that fault is sincerely recognized and accepted…that you step up and take accountability for your actions," says author and coach Gary Ryan Blair, creator of the 100 Day Challenge. "An excuse exists to justify, blame or defend a fault…with the intent to absolve oneself of accountability."

Usually, you'll have an explanation for not having done something: you had a long day at work; the kids required more energy and time than expected; your knee was acting up. Any of these can be a reason or an excuse. Look inside yourself and examine the explanation honestly. Can you take accountability and address the cause(s) so that you don't experience the pain or frustration again in the future?

You might even be able to reframe the issue in a positive way: "Yeah, the trash didn't go out, but I had awesome quality time with my friends instead, and that's worth the possibility that the trash might smell today!"

This sort of consciousness-shifting can be powerful. Whether the examination leads to changed behavior or to an awareness of the reason and being okay with it, it can help take you out of a victimhood mentality. Breaking out of that mentality—which involves ongoing shame, guilt, and pain—can help set you up to make future choices from a more empowered place. Instead of saying, "I'm horrible for not taking the trash out," you might shift the dialogue to "I made the choice to hang out with friends. The trash will go out tomorrow, and that's okay," or "I did not set myself up for success schedule-wise. Next time I'll take out the trash before I leave for my friends' house."

Most of us are doing the best we can with the choices we have available to us or the awareness we have in each moment. Examination is not about faulting ourselves if we didn't have access to other choices in a specific moment. It may even help us become aware of circumstances we were not previously conscious of. Perhaps you realize you are mad at yourself because your parents yelled at you about the same issue when you were a kid—that your response is based on an external individual whose own responses previously caused you harm.

Self-compassion is important in these awareness-building exercises. It can take active processing with a therapist, spiritual advisor, coach, best friend, or partner to deeply examine and work through these. Some people may also want to address underlying situations first, such as domestic violence or substance use.

> When looking at your "whys," you might uncover a secondary benefit from a certain behavior. Someone I know was trying to quit smoking but couldn't make it click. They promised themself they would quit. They tried a variety of programs to address the primary benefit of smoking—a nicotine high—with no luck. They even tried meds, and still, they kept smoking, especially at work.
>
> One day, it hit them. They worked a very high-stress job, and smokers were the only people being guaranteed their break times by management. A part of the person's unconscious mind was holding on to smoking for its secondary purpose—gaining break time—and they needed to build new systems to meet that secondary need before they could quit. Their mind was taking care of itself, but the form that was taking was also causing physical and emotional harm.
>
> If you find yourself unable to break a self-harming habit, look beyond the surface for any secondary benefits rather than talking to yourself cruelly about it. Oftentimes, our mind is trying to support us in getting what we need and is using the tools at hand. Figuring out these secondary benefits can help you determine and look for new tools to fill those needs.

KNOWING OUR "WHYS"

You might find externalizing "why" questions helpful, phrasing them as if you were asking someone else. Instead of asking, "Why didn't I go put socks on when my feet were cold?" ask, "Why didn't they put their socks on when their feet were cold?" This can give you space to have the empathy you might experience with others but not (yet) with yourself. You might say, "I don't know," or you might say, "They have a sore back today, and on a scale of priorities from one to ten, not moving was a seven, while putting on socks was a three."

With this information, how would you respond to the external person you were talking about? Would you say you understand? Would you ask "them" to go put their socks on now, and while up, get an ice pack so that both the seven and the three can be taken care of? Might it be an opportunity for forgiveness?

Forgiveness is not about forgetting what happened. A situation happened and resulted in consequences. Forgiveness is not an immediate cure-all. It does not wipe the slate clean. It does not immediately restore trust. This is true when we are looking to forgive ourselves, the same as when we're looking to forgive others.

Forgiving yourself is about healing yourself. It is about moving forward, one step at a time, making new decisions. Just as no one else owes you their forgiveness, though, you may have to work hard for self-forgiveness: examining your "whys," finding help, and doing the work. You can't just buy your forgiveness with a gift, hoping that the memory will go away. By changing your future behavior, you can build deeper self-love and self-trust.

Keep in mind that you don't need to soul-search every time you don't follow through on a set task! Sometimes "spoiling" yourself for one night and then changing your behavior might be exactly what you need. Perhaps you will realize that you just forgot to take out the trash, and next time you'll put a note on the door so that you remember to do so. This stuff doesn't have to always be soul-draining. In fact, instead of being exhausting, the process of moving out of self-hurt and broken self-promises and into self-forgiveness can be a delight.

If one week you didn't follow through on a planned task and the next week you do the planned task, give yourself some praise! Good for you for remembering. If you do a weekly task for five weeks in a row and then forget during the sixth week, you'll have five weeks of positivity to outweigh the one week of forgetting and can say to yourself, "Yup, I forgot, but I've proven that I can do it most of the time. Go me!" Not only can you get back on the horse, but you can get back on with pride.

Prizes are a great motivator for some people. If you are wired this way, consider what kind of prize might motivate you to complete a task or accomplish a goal—such as indulging in a treat, buying yourself flowers, or having an erotic night with yourself. You might even want to give yourself a literal gold star—stickers can be a big motivator, even for adults.

What we don't need in the midst of struggle is shame for being human. —Brené Brown

As you move forward, remember to stay focused on the now instead of slipping into associated stories from the past. Being mindful of current realities and experiences can go a long way toward forgiveness and self-evolution. Rooting yourself in the past can be a form of hurting or retraumatizing yourself, carrying suffering long after the issue is gone.

Today is a new day, even if an issue might look like something from the past. Today brings new information and allows you to make new decisions. Moving forward from a place of compassion for yourself, and in turn the world, will allow you to evolve and make the world a better place.

Remember, forgiveness is not about blame. Forgiveness is about apology, understanding, compassion, healing, making new choices, and moving forward.

✧ Exercise: Practice Forgiveness

In this exercise, you will take one thing you would like to have you forgive yourself for. Make your answers specific, which will create more impact. Make sure the part of you doing this exercise is writing (or saying) words that the part of you that was negatively affected will hear or receive.

If you're listening to this in audiobook form, you can download the written worksheet at http://www.passionandsoul.com/beloved.

Remember: with each of the exercises in this book, you get to choose if and how to engage with them. The choice is always yours.

1. Set aside ten to fifteen minutes for this exercise.
2. Acquire a writing utensil that feels good in your hand.

3. Shake out your body. Stretch your arms, wiggle your toes, and let go of the stories and stresses of the day for a moment. This is a moment for you to listen to *you*.
4. Take three deep breaths. With the first, breathe in, and release. With the second, breathe in, and release with a longer breath out. With the third, take a deep breath, filling up your body from your toes up to your nose, hold for a moment, and release until your shoulders drop. Repeat that last one if needed.
5. Think of something that you did to yourself that you are sorry about and would like forgiveness for. Remember to make it specific, like "I did not take out the trash today." Write it down here:

_____

6. State your apology. Write an "I am sorry…" or "I apologize for…" statement regarding the issue:

_____

7. State your understanding of why the action that needs to be forgiven took place. Write an "I understand that…" or "It is understandable that…" statement regarding the issue. This is not about blame; it is showing yourself that you understand why it happened:

_____

8. State what might need to be healed from the situation that you are seeking forgiveness for. Write a "Because of my actions…" or "I understand that…" statement regarding what happened because of your behaviors or actions:

_____

9. State the new choices or actions you will be taking. Write one to three actionable steps that will set you up for success in the future:

_____

10. Sit with yourself. Look at the answers above. How do you feel about what you had to say? What do you think about it? Do any pieces need examining or amending?

_____

11. Do you choose to forgive yourself? If yes, write that you forgive yourself, stating specifically what you are forgiving yourself for:

_____

12. If forgiving yourself does not feel authentic, what can you write instead? If it is a request that you do the actions promised, perhaps you might begin, "Once you do the actions promised..." Be authentic and be honest with yourself when both "speaking" and "listening":

_____

13. Thank yourself for doing the work.

Adaptations

If you have dyslexia, dysgraphia, or a vision impairment, or do not enjoy doing writing-based exercises, you can download the audio file at http://www.passionandsoul.com/beloved.

Once you've downloaded it, you can answer the questions in a few different ways:

A. Write your answers on paper with your chosen writing instrument.
B. Type your answers out on your computer and save them for later.
C. Audio- or video-record your answers on a smartphone, computer, or other device.
D. Answer out loud.
E. Answer in your head.

Going Forward

If you did not forgive yourself in step 11, come back to this exercise in the next few days to repeat steps 1–10 with something "smaller." This is not always an easy process. Starting with something that you do not consider a big deal can help build up the muscle of forgiveness, in all its steps, over time.

If you did forgive yourself in step 11, consider reflecting on or writing about how this practice of forgiveness has helped you heal and move forward in your life. This can include a statement of compassion for yourself about how you not only understand what happened but have compassion for the person who made that decision or action. Celebrate the healed parts of you and your ability to evolve!

Chapter 9

THE JUGGLING ACT: BALANCING OTHER RELATIONSHIPS

Many of us believe that we are not enough on our own, that we need someone to complete us. This story from the Cult of the Couple states that we are lacking in some way unless we have our "other half" or "better half." We are part of a whole that is missing our other part if we are not partnered with another person.

But what if relationships were about being whole people rather than fractional ones?

You are a whole being. So is every person you meet.

Your self-worth is determined by you. You don't have to depend on someone telling you who you are. —BEYONCÉ KNOWLES

Every relationship with someone else is composed of three relationships. You have a relationship with yourself (relationship A). The other person has a relationship with themself (relationship B). Then there is the relationship the two of you share with each other (relationship AB).

Being in relationship with others is about acknowledging, maintaining, and supporting all three of these relationships. This is true no matter the shape of the relationship: friend, family member, spouse, partner, coworker, peer, or acquaintance. In fact, we have many relationships in the world, based on each connection that we form. Not only is there A, B, and AB, but also A, C, and AC, and so on. This is why so many folks work to balance their time and energy between their best friends and their romantic partners, because relationships B and C both matter to them.

NEW RELATIONSHIP ENERGY

When we're in relationships that are fresh to us, new relationship energy, or NRE, might cause us to forget our relationship with ourselves. With NRE, everything feels exciting. The rest of the world often melts away, and our mind becomes centered on exuberance, fascination, and even obsession with the fresh connection. This can happen with a new romantic connection, a new friendship, a new coworker who shares our passions for a project, or any interpersonal dynamic.

This sort of energy can lead us to forget our relationship with ourselves as well as our other existing relationships, including friendships, family bonds, career connections, and more. We focus on the new AB relationship, and the other person forgets their relationship with themself as well.

New relationship energy is rich and enjoyable, but maintaining our relationships with others and ourselves allows that new relationship to be stronger and more stable. Instead of seeing our relationship with ourselves as an "either-or" choice compared to our various external relationships, we are building allyship and depth. Love is not a pie with a fixed number of slices where we must choose how many slices each person gets. Instead, it is a system by which the more each person brings to the table, the easier it is for everyone to feast.

This means that we get to maintain our self-love and self-connection to help our relationships with others thrive. It also means that others get to maintain their self-love and self-connection to help their relationships with us thrive. All three of these relationships need to be fed.

> My former spouse and I both enjoyed live action role-playing games. We would dress up in costumes and play various characters, going out every weekend to enjoy this fun way of stepping away from the stress of day-to-day life.
>
> After spending the night at a game, we would come home and start talking about everything we had gotten up to. We would share stories, laughing as we debriefed from the event, and take the time to thoughtfully listen to what each other had gotten out of going out. One night, it struck me. We had each had our own individual time and then come together to connect with each other.

My spouse had fed their relationship with themself by having a chance to do deep role exploration, play with the tactics of war games, and have an immersive experience. I had fed my relationship with myself by doing improv theater, delighting in playing dress-up, and having time between scenes to catch up with friends. Together, we reconnected through the act of storytelling, something we both deeply enjoyed. One evening out had fed our three relationships, with our celebrating each other's nights rather than holding any judgment. Delight, respect, and curiosity had led us to deepening our support for each other's evenings and our connection with each other.

THE PLATINUM RULE

Each person's self-knowledge and self-connection will look different because everyone is unique. Don't compare your connection with yourself to how another person connects to themself. It might be tempting to tell someone that they need to go take a bubble bath and have some solo quiet time—after all, that helps you, right? But that person might be fed by going out and playing hockey with their friends, having self-love time through sweat and extroversion.

The Golden Rule is imperfect. It says, "do unto others as you want done unto you." The Platinum Rule is far more useful. Do unto others as they want done.

A friend, family member, or partner might mean well by saying you should go play sports with friends, when what you want is quiet time with no one else around. This is not because they mean ill. It means they are trying to support your relationship with yourself or your relationships with others. That is wonderful! They just missed the mark. Doing your own version of self-love and self-knowing work can allow you to be confident in knowing what types of support you need from yourself and other sources rather than what someone else is projecting upon you based on their own life and needs.

The same is true when you are trying to "help" others. Not everyone is supported in their self-love in the same way you are. You may enjoy a date night with your journal to self-reflect, while your sibling may spend time with their therapist to do the same. Both of you are supporting your internal relationships, and by doing so, hopefully leveling up your shared relationship as siblings over time.

Listen to how the person you are in relationship with talks about the type of actions you should be doing to feel supported. This is often a clue as to the sort of care they might want to be giving themselves. Having awareness of their needs for self-support can provide a tool for offering them ideas when they are in need.

Asking someone we are in a relationship with what self-support they enjoy can be a powerful relationship bonding tool. You can have a list of things they like for themselves, and they can have a list of things you like doing for yourself. When they want more self-time, you have ideas to offer for activities that would be desired by them (the Platinum Rule) rather than ones that you're projecting on them (the Golden Rule). Learning more about each other allows for deeper relationship building as well, no matter the shape of the relationship.

Sometimes, the people we are with have never had a chance to consider these questions. These conversations become a chance to have an ally in self-connection. Make pacts with your loved ones to do the work and delight of the Self. Whether they are willing or able to participate in the joy and challenge of self-connection also becomes information about what energy they are bringing to your shared relationship. Ask yourself what draws you to them and perhaps what draws them to you. Gathering this combination of information is a way to thrive as well.

> Codependency Says: "Doing the work" with a partner means betraying or denying parts of myself.
>
> Interdependency Says: "Doing the work" in a relationship also means doing the work in the most important relationship I'll ever have: the one with myself. —Dr. Nicole LePera

RELATIONSHIPS CHANGE SHAPE

When each of us does our own self-work, it will affect our shared relationships. If relationship A changes its shape, whether relationship B changes its shape or not, AB will inherently change its shape because relationship A is part of it. If relationships A and B both evolve, AB will shape-shift even more.

When you, in relationship A, look at AB, it might not resemble the original shared relationship you began with or agreed to. That does not make the new AB wrong. It means that A, B, or AB has evolved, and you might want to make new decisions about how you commit to or invest in the relationship. AB has evolved because every relationship evolves and each of us as individuals evolves. This can even be a chance for NRE to spring up anew. However, it can also mean that a new shape of AB needs to exist, or partners need to untangle from the former AB that existed.

If your relationship with yourself changes, it will affect your relationships with others. Conversely, if your relationships with others change, it will affect your relationship with yourself. Because of this, it's important to be conscious, when forming relationships of all sorts with others, to take care of yourself. Not only is this about asking who the other people are—exploring their life, labels, and self-identity—but it's also about asking how they relate to you.

Ask yourself: Do they like you, or do they want to have a relationship with someone to fill a perceived lack in their life? Do they see who you are, or are they painting a picture of you that matches their needs, wants, and desires? After all, it is possible to be lonely while in a relationship.

INTERNAL AND EXTERNAL AUTHENTICITY

Being externally authentic is important for having people "see" us, but not everyone is in a place of safety, trust, courage, or self-knowledge to share their authentic Self with others. To do so, we need to begin with being authentic with ourselves.

BECOME YOUR OWN BELOVED

Are you authentic to yourself? Internal authenticity is about being true to your values, personality, and internal truths, no matter what external influences might come along. External authenticity is letting others see that authentic Self and is sometimes read as "not caring what other people think." However, for many people, especially those of various disenfranchised or oppressed populations, external authenticity is not always viable, lest they lose their job, home, children, and more.

> You're always with yourself, so you might as well enjoy the company. —Diane von Furstenberg

Doing the work in this book is about building up care for your internal authentic Self, whether you express it externally for everyone to see or not. You are not being less authentic if you do not express everything externally. You can be true to your values, internal truths, and core personality however you show yourself to the world.

Sexuality educator Diamond Blue argues that each of us has many aspects of ourselves that can be authentic or inauthentic. Each of us has many sides after all. The side of you that shows up as a parent will not look the same as the side of you that shows up as a lover. The side of you that shows up as a coworker will not look the same as the side of you that shows up with your closest friends.

With this being true, it means that when some people see us in different sides of our life, they might think we have been inauthentic with them. However, what it usually means is that we show different sides of ourselves as multifaceted beings. Some people may also choose to be externally authentic with some sides of themselves, and externally inauthentic with others. They may be internally authentic but are not sharing all their sides as a form of self-protection or way to maintain privacy.

Assess the different sides of yourself. You may find you are internally authentic in some, externally authentic in others, and inauthentic in a few. This sort of self-assessment can become a powerful tool for deciding how healthy each of your relationships are for you.

✧ Exercise: Examine New Relationship Energy

In this exercise, you will examine how new relationship energy appears in your life and how you can have more success feeding yourself within those relationships—whether they are social, romantic, professional, sexual, or some other type.

If you're listening to this in audiobook form, you can download the written worksheet at http://www.passionandsoul.com/beloved.

Remember: with each of the exercises in this book, you get to choose if and how to engage with them. The choice is always yours.

1. Set aside ten to fifteen minutes for this exercise. If you only have a few minutes here and there, that's okay—just pause the exercise whenever you need to.

2. Acquire a writing utensil that feels good in your hand.
3. Shake out your body. Stretch your arms, wiggle your toes, and let go of the stories and stresses of the day for a moment.
4. Take three deep breaths. With the first, breathe in, and release. With the second, breathe in, and release with a longer breath out. With the third, take a deep breath, filling up your body from your toes up to your nose, hold for a moment, and release until your shoulders drop. Repeat that last one if needed.
5. Once your shoulders have dropped, begin the worksheet. Look at the first question and seriously consider it.
6. Take a breath (or as long of a break as needed) and then answer the question in its entirety before moving on to the next question. If you do not have an answer to a question, draw a line under it or write that you do not have an answer currently. There are no right answers, including not having an answer, and you can have different answers if you do this exercise on a different day.
7. Set the worksheet aside. Stand up, stretch out your body, drink some water, or take some sort of other short, non-stressful break.
8. Come back to your answers and decide on one action step you will take this week to ask for an expression of care or provide an action of care.
9. Thank yourself for doing the work.

Adaptations

If you have dyslexia, dysgraphia, or a vision impairment, or do not enjoy doing writing-based exercises, you can download the audio file at http://www.passionandsoul.com/beloved. Once you've downloaded it, you can answer the questions in a few different ways:

A. Write your answers on paper with your chosen writing instrument.
B. Type your answers out on your computer and save them for later.
C. Audio- or video-record your answers on a smartphone, computer, or other device.
D. Answer out loud.
E. Answer in your head.

Worksheet

A. Choose one connection you are deeply drawn to or are passionate about right now. This could be a coworker, romantic relationship, friendship, hobby partner, social connection online, fellow activist, lover, family member, or someone else entirely. (If you cannot think of one currently, consider reflecting on a past relationship, and know that listing one relationship does not make another relationship less important in your life.)

B. In what ways is new relationship energy manifesting with this individual?

_____

C. How is the relationship with this individual adding to your relationship with yourself?

_____

D. How is the relationship with this individual detracting or distracting from your relationship with yourself?

_____

E. What, specifically, is one way that you have shown up for that relationship with one of the neurodivergent or classic love languages (from chapter 5)?

_____

F. What, specifically, is one way that you can show up for that relationship with one of the love languages that you have not done so yet?

_____

G. What, specifically, is one way that the other person has shown up for that relationship with one of the love languages?

___

H. What, specifically, is one way that this individual can show up for that relationship with one of the love languages that they have not done so yet.

___

Going Forward

If, at the end of the week, you were not able to do or receive the expressions of care you noted in the final step, be gentle with yourself. Do not use "should" when talking with yourself. This is not a competition, and there is nothing wrong with having prioritized other things during the week of this exercise.

Take a chance instead to reflect on the week and see if you did anything to show this person love, appreciation, or support, or if you asked for or created situations where they could provide you with the same. Seemingly little things from others can help us build up how we relate to ourselves and caring for others can remind us how we also want to care for ourselves.

If you don't have a new relationship, hobby, passion, or connection currently, consider returning to this exercise when you do. You'll garner another layer of self-knowledge by noticing the differences between your previous and new answers.

Chapter 10

YOU ARE NOT ALONE: TAPPING INTO COMMUNITY SUPPORT

We form relationships not just with individuals but with and within social groups or communities. We are all part of larger social networks, whether we consciously realize it or not, and pretending otherwise will not help us thrive as individuals. Idolizing the lone-wolf model of being with only ourselves can be just as toxic as the Cult of the Couple model discussed in the introduction and removes us from the richness that a culture of mutual support can provide each of us.

Many of the ideas and questions in the last chapter can apply to a community as well. The community could be a hobby group, school, fandom, barber shop, business, club, band, religious group, team, or something else. It might be your family of blood, multi-partnered relationship, or some other family of choice. Perhaps it is your friendship circle.

Caring for others is important, but Covid-19 taught us that sometimes, by caring for yourself, you're caring for others, too." —Becca Kaye, senior care specialist at AvaCare Medical

Some are rich and thriving. The various internal parts work well with each other, and the people within are thriving under its behaviors, ethics, structure, and cultural norms. The group as a whole is a cohesive entity whose members flow well with each other. When there is strife, there is a system in place that helps all its parts come together to heal and grow from that strife.

Other communities have toxic dynamics and an internal structure that is harmful to its members and to the group as a whole. Not all communities are healthy and worth joining. When you're considering joining a community, look closely at both the dynamics and the structure to make sure you will truly thrive instead of being harmed. Consider dipping in a toe before jumping in whole hog, as initial appearances can be deceiving—especially if you're being "recruited." Talk with people who've been in the community a while to get their perspective.

COMMUNITY RELATIONSHIP FORMULAS

The first way to look at our relationships in a group or community is to extend the equation from the previous chapter. Three people end up having seven relationships—A, B, C,

AB, AC, BC, and ABC. Four people have fifteen relationships—A, B, C, D, AB, AC, AD, BC, BD, CD, ABC, ABD, ACD, BCD…and ABCD as a single entity. Interpersonal relationships, when examined holistically, are exponential mathematics.

The other route is to think of the entire community as one entity. In this case, we think of our relationship with ourselves as relationship A. The community or group we are involved with, relationship B, has the internal dynamics and social norms as well. Relationship AB is then how we relate to that group.

In the context of community, self-love can take many forms. This is especially true for individuals who want to provide acts of service, where serving the community creates an internal sense of delight. In this case, loving yourself is what helps strengthen your joy in a parallel way to supporting our partners in their sense of joy. Volunteering for events, being there for a friend when they are feeling down, stepping into leadership roles, and backing community actions raise up not just relationship A but relationship AB as well. Everyone thrives.

> Be kinder to yourself. And then let your kindness flood the world. —PEMA CHÖDRÖN

However, there is a difference between giving acts of service and being taken for granted. Asking when the last time your community supported you can be hard sometimes but is important. Some groups that call themselves communities are one-way streets when it comes to the energy offered. That does not mean being part of those communities is inherently unhealthy for you—it means it is worth the self-interrogation of the situation.

BUILDING HEALTHY BOUNDARIES

Looking at relationships where you give but get little or nothing in return can also be an opportunity to build boundaries or frameworks. These are two tools that become a useful pair by pointing out not just what we do not want, but what we desire as well.

Former lawyer and life coach Olivia Vizachero breaks down the concept of boundaries in a clear way, stating, "Boundaries are not mandates for other people to follow." Instead, Vizachero offers that, "It's a particular course of action YOU take to take care of yourself when a particular set of circumstances arises. That's it. It's about what YOU do. Not about what THEY do. Ever." A statement that someone needs to treat you better is not a boundary. Instead, a boundary would be "I will leave if you raise your voice again."

Boundaries give our conscious mind a place where we can be aware that we thrive on one side of the boundary and not on the other, but more than that, developing boundaries allows us to know what we will do if that line is crossed. Boundaries become a tool of empowerment so that we know our path ahead rather than someone else setting them for us. By knowing for ourselves what will happen, boundaries are a tool for succeeding in our interactions with others and keeping us out of the way of abuse and other kinds of harm when we are interacting with partners or groups.

Frameworks in turn are a way we can say that we will build off our "yesses" rather than following our "nos." What brings you delight? What would help you succeed? Frameworks help us actively create a life of our dreams, rather than only spending our energy and focus on what does not serve us. They give us a compass to point towards our desires.

Being aware of our frameworks and boundaries helps us care for ourselves by having others, and ourselves, respect our autonomy. Clarifying our boundaries to them provides a space for mutual respect through you respecting their boundaries in turn. If a friend sets a boundary and you respect it, this respect becomes part of a beautiful web where everyone supports each other's needs, wants, and desires.

> There is only one corner of the universe you can be certain of improving, and that is your own self. So you have to begin there, not outside, not on other people. That comes afterwards, when you have worked on your own corner.
> —Aldous Huxley

In the case of groups, having and sharing our frameworks and boundaries allows us to thrive and to know when our relationships with that group might be becoming unhealthy for us. Perhaps we tell our rugby team that we are not available for every practice. We are setting a boundary based on our life realities. In turn, our team might state that every member must attend every practice or else they cannot be part of the team. They are sharing the boundary they operate under to build up that team.

When the boundaries and frameworks of communities do not match your own, you have a choice to make in how to continue with that relationship. Perhaps you will negotiate. When coming into a discussion or negotiation, it's important to know your "hard limits" and "soft limits." These establish, within your relationship with yourself, which things you call boundaries are never to be changed and where the lines might be permeable or pliable. An actual boundary is not pliable and is a hard limit. When you state you have a boundary and show instead that it is a soft limit, it can be confusing for you as well as those you share those supposed boundaries with. Investigate your own boundary in advance. If it is flexible, it is instead a soft limit. Knowing your framework around the topic might also help in figuring out which things are hard limits, and which are soft limits.

In the case of the rugby team, an approach might be to ask the coach or team why the boundary they have is needed. In advance, you decide that practicing the number of hours requested in general is a soft limit, but the dates you need to miss are a hard limit. You ask if there might be an option to drill for the upcoming game with others who couldn't make a set practice, offering this as part of the negotiation based on your soft limit. If the coach says no, you must be there at a set time, this runs into your hard limit concerning your schedule itself. Perhaps you need to take care of your kids, have a school exam, or some other situation that makes it not pliable...or you simply do not want to. Knowing these in advance allows you to take care of yourself, relationship A, and then decide how to move forward with relationship AB.

It's also possible that the internal relationship for relationship B (the rugby team as a whole) is not in alignment with itself. Bringing up your desire for negotiation may drive relationship B to start asking itself questions it has never asked itself before. Over time, this internal work within the group may lead to a change in the group's boundaries, or a desire to shift the frameworks upon which it wants to build. They might reach out with a new desire to build a relationship with you, or you might see how they have changed and desire to connect with them anew.

Though this internal work is important in relationships with individuals, it's especially important in groups because sometimes we don't notice the changes that need to be done from inside the group when we are part of that group. Other times, we might step back until that work is done by that group and watch them carry out the change from the outside before rejoining. Your self-love and self-support come through deciding whether to help change a group from the inside, or leaving the group and seeing if it will change, having tried your best from within.

Sometimes leaving a group is difficult or problematic—for example, a family. Though some choose to leave their family of birth, others have circumstances such as children or religious beliefs that can hold back this possibility.

My mother grew up around abusive situations. The family dynamics harmed not just those who were being abused, but the abusers were perpetuating the abuse they had experienced themselves. Everyone was hurt, and as hurt people, they were hurting each other.

Even though she worked to get people out of abusive situations with groups she volunteered with, she was not willing to leave a toxic situation herself. Her internalized story based on the Cult of the Couple was that a "whole family" was inherently better than a "broken home." When I confronted her about it, she told me she was staying in this group dynamic to help me. I made it clear that being part of the group relationship called a "whole family" was harming me, and together we began planning to leave.

It took my perspective as an outsider to the situation for her to see that her desire to help others was hurting her in a way that she had not realized. Turning to a new community, one of friends and other family members, helped her leave one system to enter another. She discovered groups that could help her leave and then set up a new life for herself. It was a very hard decision for her, but the support of others made growing and then enforcing her boundaries easier. Her relationship with outside groups allowed her to build her self-confidence in ways she had not accessed before.

BENEFITS OF COMMUNITY

Groups are a powerful and delightful tool for showing us we deserve to be supported. For example, an online support network of transgender people can remind other transgender people that they are not alone. The group can share how the person deserves respect and, in doing so, remind that person to respect themself. Groups based on addiction recovery can offer support through relationships with both a sponsor and a fellowship. Church groups can offer a feeling of belonging as well as opportunities for service. Fitness groups can offer health benefits as well as camaraderie. The list goes on.

A myth exists that a person cannot be loved unless they love themself first. Though loving oneself can certainly deepen one's relationship with another person or group, sometimes external relationships can help us love ourselves. A healthy and supportive community, for example, can act as a mirror to show us that we are worthy of self-love, self-respect, and even self-delight.

One of the challenges with some approaches to individualism is that they state that if we are supporting ourselves, it is separate from supporting others. This is far from the truth. The Self is part of the whole, and the individual is part of the collective of life on this planet. If we are a leg that needs support to be able to walk, the rest of the body can support us while we also explicitly care for the leg that we are. In turn, when we are up and walking with full strength, we can take our body where it needs to be for care as a whole system.

Your self-love is a gift to those around you and your communities. Getting to know yourself is a chance to build your skillsets for knowing others. Learning how to see the complexity of your own labels lets you learn how to see the complexity of the labels for those around you. Making and keeping commitments to yourself helps you understand how to make and keep commitments to others. Your growth helps all of us grow.

> Ultimately, communities give people a supportive group to help them cope with difficult challenges, band together to solve problems, and celebrate life's lighter moments. —MAGGIE WOOL

You are already part of a group worldwide that is reading this book and doing the work to evolve and grow in themselves. You are not alone. You are worthy of self-love, self-respect, and self-delight.

✧ EXERCISE: EXAMINE COMMUNITY RELATIONSHIPS

In this exercise, you will examine how you are currently connecting with one of your communities. To do so, we will be using the model of examining our relationships with community where the community is a being whole unto itself, rather than viewing each person in the community as a separate relationship.

If you're listening to this in audiobook form, you can download the written worksheet at http://www.passionandsoul.com/beloved.

Remember: with each of the exercises in this book, you get to choose if and how to engage with them. The choice is always yours.

1. Set aside ten to fifteen minutes for this exercise. If you only have a few minutes here and there, that's okay—just pause the exercise whenever you need to.
2. Acquire a writing utensil that feels good in your hand.
3. Shake out your body. Stretch your arms, wiggle your toes, and let go of the stories and stresses of the day for a moment.
4. Take three deep breaths. With the first, breathe in, and release. With the second, breathe in, and release with a longer breath out. With the third, take a deep breath, filling up your body from your toes up to your nose, hold for a moment, and release until your shoulders drop. Repeat that last one if needed.
5. Once your shoulders have dropped, begin the worksheet. Look at the first question and seriously consider it.
6. Take a breath (or as long of a break as needed) and then answer the question in its entirety before moving on to the next question. If you do not have an answer to a question, draw a line under it or write that you do not have an answer currently. There are no right answers, including not having an answer, and you can have different answers if you do this exercise on a different day.
7. Set the worksheet aside. Stand up, stretch out your body, drink some water, or take some sort of other short, non-stressful break.

8. Come back to your answers and decide if you want to take one of the questions into being an action step over the next week.
9. Thank yourself for doing the work.

Adaptations

If you have dyslexia, dysgraphia, or a vision impairment, or do not enjoy doing writing-based exercises, you can download the audio file at http://www.passionandsoul.com/beloved.

Once you've downloaded it, you can answer the questions in a few different ways:

A. Write your answers on paper with your chosen writing instrument.
B. Type your answers out on your computer and save them for later.
C. Audio- or video-record your answers on a smartphone, computer, or other device.
D. Answer out loud.
E. Answer in your head.

Worksheet

A. Make a list of which communities you are currently part of. These communities could include a group, school, fandom, business, club, band, religious group, team, friendship circle, family of blood, multi-partnered relationship, family of choice, or something else entirely.

B. Choose one relationship from this list. (If you cannot think of any that you are currently part of, consider reflecting on a past community, and know that listing one community does not make another community less important in your life.)

_____

C. How does that community help you thrive as an individual?

_____

D. What is one action you can do to be more enriched in that community?

_____

E. What is one way you can give back to that community?

_____

F. What is one challenge you are having or have had in that community?

_____

G. What is one way that community can give back to you?

_____

H. How can you communicate that to the members of that community?

_____

I. How can you help yourself be more rooted in that community?

_____

Going Forward

If you said you were going to follow an action step as noted in the final step, at the end of the week check in with yourself. Did you follow that action step, or instead give yourself space to not do so at this time? Be gentle with yourself. Do not use "should" when talking with yourself. This is not a competition, and there is nothing wrong with having prioritized other things or changing your mind.

Whether you chose to follow an action step or not on step 8, read through your original answers. Have you changed your mind or had additional thoughts to add? This is a chance to reflect on where and how you are situated in this group as well as how and if you might be interested in changing the place you are oriented therein.

Consider coming back to this exercise at some point with another group in mind if you find yourself in a place of conflict or uncertainty with your relationship to that group. New information can often be garnered by doing so, as can more insight into how your answers compare for different groups you are part of. Are there parallels, or are your relationships to different groups unique?

Chapter 11

MAINTENANCE NEEDS: KEEPING UP WITH COMFORT AND CARE

Learning about yourself is a gift not just to yourself, but to the world. Showing up in your power encourages others to do the same. It also helps you reside in your skin rather than dissociate, make choices about where you want to invest your time and energy, and delight in the joy you have around you—all of which can be inspiring. When you tune into the desires of your own beloved, yourself, you are more likely to make choices that will help you thrive. Modeling that can motivate others to make healthy choices as well.

Even with that knowledge, some days I do not embrace or embody that power. That's okay. Every day, we can do the work again. We can remember how to self-delight, how to be peaceful through self-actions, how to feel self-supported. As with any relationship, our relationships with ourselves will have their ups and downs, twists and turns. Without the downs, we wouldn't know how to recognize the ups. Without the twists and turns, we might not notice the complexities of being human.

> Caring for myself is not self-indulgence, it is self-preservation, and that is an act of political warfare. —AUDRE LORDE

In a busy world, taking time to work on yourself can feel overwhelming, selfish, and like a low priority. Love may be infinite, but time is not. However, you and your relationship with yourself are worth the energy and ongoing investment. Finding the time and space for your own upkeep is one of the greatest gifts you can give yourself and others around you.

SELF-CARE THAT SERVES YOU

Part of your relationship upkeep is self-care. This term is overused in our culture and stripped down to a pastel-colored advertisement of women in bubble baths or on expensive yoga retreats. Capitalism has wedged its way into how we love ourselves through practical action. It is time for us to take the concept back.

For some people, self-care *is* about fuzzy blankets, spa days, and freshly baked cookies. For others, it's decompressing in a martial arts class or on the ice with hockey stick in hand. Self-care takes a thousand forms. When you're trying to figure out what self-care practices will serve you best, consider what soothes you, rejuvenates you, or energizes you. Consider activities that you actively delight in as well as quietly rest in.

Do you relish naps, rest, quiet, and solitude? Are you moved to go to the nail salon or watch a soccer game? Does your body dwell in relaxation as you work on your car or craft project? Is your self-care sensual jazz, Bollywood beats, or ferocious metal? Is it minding your social media hygiene by unsubscribing from certain accounts or adding inspiring quote and art providers to your feed?

These practices will not guarantee you will feel good. But they are tools to help upkeep your relationship with yourself as you navigate the world at large.

Remember: if you don't keep up with your self-care, you can always start again. A self-care practice is called a *practice* for a reason.

ROUTES OF SAFETY

For examining and crafting your self-care practice, the Routes of Safety can be a powerful aid. Developed by Jake Ernst, MSW, the Routes of Safety are eight ways anyone can use to move toward feeling safe. Feeling safe is key in building trust, finding balance, and doing the work of healing, whether relating to ourselves or others. Safety is the foundation for helping us not just survive but delight in our life at large.

The eight Routes of Safety are:
- Inner Guidance
- Structure and Certainty
- Sensory Experiences

- ◆ Quality Relationships
- ◆ Closeness and Proximity
- ◆ Private Retreat
- ◆ Protective Measures
- ◆ Common Humanity

Some of these will resonate for you more than others. Some might do the opposite of helping you feel safe or experience support, and instead cause feelings of stress, frustration, depression, and more. Listen to your body, mind, and spirit. You are unique, and your systems of care should fit who you really are.

> Remember always that you not only have the right to be an individual, you have an obligation to be one. —ELEANOR ROOSEVELT

If your Route of Safety is *Inner Guidance*, tools like writing and journaling can be wonderful for self-examination. Cultivating presence, mindfulness, grounding, and meditation can help with relaxation and rejuvenation alike. By building self-compassion, self-trust, and the capacity to feel deep and energizing feelings, this route can help you soothe you or reframe how you see the world and yourself.

Along the route of *Structure and Certainty*, self-care can look like cleaning, organizing, or clearing out your closets. You might center yourself by making lists and schedules, getting everything in your world flowing in a more formal manner. Making rituals and systems might help you on your path of staying busy and finding certainty in an uncertain world. Having something to do, rather than resting, might feel good to you.

The route of *Sensory Experiences* taps into all the work of chapter 6. Watching clouds, listening to nature, and taking deep breaths of smells that light you up can help you tap into your authentic Self. In deeply savoring each bite of food or sip of tea, you ground into your body, letting yourself be nourished, relaxed, and relieved. If this is you, everything from cuddling a pet to fully delighting in delicious sex can help bring you into a place of equilibrium.

Having *Quality Relationships* is a Route of Safety embedded in how we connect with others. Coregulation, healing, and attunement with people we care about helps us feel stable, whether we're in a relationship or dealing with the world at large. Feeling close to community becomes important, and building connections with new people or established friends can be powerful. This can include intimate touch, playfulness, breathing while looking in someone else's eyes, or having people cheer you on in life. If this is your route you cannot follow it in a vacuum. A wide array of connections, or a few deep ones, will be greatly beneficial in your self-care.

Closeness and Proximity as a Route of Safety is about more than just the love language of touch. Yes, it can include giving or receiving touch of all sorts, from sharing hugs and lying across someone's lap to holding hands or spending time in the bedroom. But it can also involve feeling secure and protected just knowing someone is available when stressful times come up. If this route speaks to you, being held, swaddled, kissed, or simply being in the room with someone supportive can help you feel more safe, alive, and energized.

Conversely, people who want quiet or alone time often look to *Private Retreat* as their Route of Safety. Being home alone, including spending time immersed in art, music, or books, helps them regain balance. If this sounds like you, you might enjoy spending time in the darkness of an unlit room, spending time outside at night, or in cozy spaces. Emotional distance can also help you feel safe; perhaps you even dissociate when physical escape is not available. If so, your desire for emotional distance is a tactic of self-preservation, intended not to harm others but rather to care for yourself.

Perhaps you find safety and practice self-care through *Protective Measures*. Cultivating self-sufficiency, pragmatism, and physical protection can help with this. You also might thrive by setting boundaries with others, finding people you can be radically honest or vulnerable with, or connecting with people who have the tools necessary for restorative justice and reconciliation. You also might find comfort and security by setting yourself up with quality survival strategies, knowing you'll be set up for worst-case scenarios.

The final Route of Safety is that of finding *Common Humanity* with others. By being seen, heard, and recognized by others, those who embrace this route know that, like all people, they are imperfect and still connected with the people around them. If this is you, your sense of safety will be supported by being listened to and believed when you share thoughts and experiences, and when others share these with you. Opportunities to share joy and play can be just as important as sharing the challenges of life; your connections with others are what's key.

> Just because you don't require a lot in order to be happy doesn't mean you deserve only the bare minimum. —ADAM HAMILL

HEARING THE WISDOM OF YOUR BODY

Nurturing ourselves goes beyond cognitive practices and theory. It involves listening to the wisdom of our bodies. Our bodies let us know when we feel balanced, grounded, and safe, as well as when we feel stressed, scattered, and unsafe.

For example, perhaps some of the exercises in this book made your shoulders push up toward your ears or your belly clench up. Perhaps some made you smile or sigh in relief. Your body holds wisdom that your conscious thinking sometimes doesn't pick up on. Learning to listen to your body can be a powerful tool in figuring out what does and does not serve you. Sometimes your brain will try to tell you things that your body knows to be untrue. In those cases, listening to your body is an act of respecting your beloved, yourself.

This is one reason that, throughout the exercises in this book, I have asked you to wait to do an exercise until your shoulders have dropped. Many people unconsciously carry stress by tensing their shoulders; it can feel like carrying a backpack of worries and fears. Setting down one fear, even if just for five minutes, can help that backpack feel lighter.

You can start learning to heed this somatic wisdom by paying attention to where you carry stress in your body. Do you clench your jaw when you are frustrated? Tighten up your calves or thighs? Do you curl up your toes or flare your nose? Do you push your tongue to the back of your teeth or cramp up your abs?

To let go of the stress wherever you find it, you might massage those areas. Perhaps you can consciously release your shoulders or dance your midsection into feeling looser. Actively clenching and then fully letting go in the areas can be a useful tool as well. There are as many ways to release bodily stress as there are kinds of stress!

Listening to your body also includes paying attention to *when* this stress manifested itself. When did your shoulders go up? What was happening around you? When did you clench our jaw? What did you or someone around you say? When did you curl up your toes? Had certain smells or sounds just wafted into the room?

Conversely, note instances of delight in your body. What physical expressions does your body make when you are happy? Comfortable? Playful? Peaceful? Loving? How do joy, relief, and relaxation express themselves in your body?

This begins the process of building an internal map of the power and beauty you carry. Instead of noticing each part of your body to look for stress, try doing one for an emotion that is delicious to you. If you bring awareness first to your feet, then legs, then pelvis, then midsection—where do you experience happiness? Hilarity? Softness? Strength? Seeing where you are holding these in your body can help the process of spreading those sensations as well as examining what your body is doing when experiencing those concepts and feelings. If you know you feel power in your softness at the same time your hands are loose and open, it creates an opportunity to open and loosen your hands when wanting to evoke that emotion from within.

Thus, there are two major ways to listen to your body. The first is to notice your body doing something it does not normally do, then ask yourself what emotion you are feeling. Are you feeling unsafe, anxious, joyous, or cheerful? The second is, when you're having an emotion you can clearly label, to examine how your body is responding. Are your eyebrows up or your shoulders slumped forward? Is your chest tight or your belly feeling relaxed? Neither way of learning to listen to the wisdom of your body is any better or worse, of course. You can use one or both as best serves you.

When I accept myself, I am freed from the burden of needing you to accept me.
—Dr. Steve Maraboli

"HACKING" THE BRAIN-BODY RELATIONSHIP

By learning what your body does when you're in an enjoyable headspace, you can then start "hacking" your brain-to-body relationship. I know, for example, that when my shoulders are down, I am likely in a calmer state of mind. When in a calmer state of mind, I can listen to and answer questions with more clarity. Thus, if I want to have more clarity, I will take a deep breath, lower my shoulders, and let that breath go. I team up with my body to reach a goal that will serve me, my friend, my beloved. It is the equivalent of giving a partner a massage when they are stressed—my partner just happens to be me.

These hacks might not be about what you can do inside your body, but what you can do *with* your body. This could include physically leaving a space you are in—changing your environment. Maybe it looks like going for a walk or a wheelchair outing, dancing at a club or meditating in a different room or enjoying any of the activities from Chapter 6 or 7.

Your relationship between your heart and your mind can help you learn self-connection for a life of love and delight. The relationship between these and your body is just as important, though, and keeping them all connected will help you maintain self-delight in your life moving forward. After all, they are not truly three separate things but rather all interwoven into you, your Self.

✧ Exercise: Express Your Routes of Safety

Here you'll figure out which Routes of Safety resonate with you the most. Perhaps you were taught by your family, friends, or culture that some of these are better than others. You might have heard that some of these are negative ways to achieve a sense of safety, comfort, balance, or care. Consciously try to set those preconceived notions aside as you go through this worksheet.

After you write your answers, you'll practice some of the routes to find out which ones might serve you best.

If you're listening to this in audiobook form, you can download the written worksheet at http://www.passionandsoul.com/beloved.

Remember: with each of the exercises in this book, you get to choose if and how to engage with them. The choice is always yours.

1. Write down each of the Routes of Safety on a page of paper or use the worksheet.
2. Go back through this chapter and use the examples provided as a starting point to brainstorm a few ideas for each of these Routes of Safety for reaching emotional equilibrium, balance, safety, security, or harmony. For each route, write down one to four ideas for things you might enjoy experiencing from yourself or experiencing for yourself.
3. Set down the list for five to ten minutes and come back to look at the list with fresh eyes.
4. Put a star next to a total of five of these that you can commit to doing in the next week. You will not have a star in every Route of Safety.

5. Remember to set yourself up for success—promising yourself to go on a weekend-long silent retreat, if you know you must care for your children this week, might not be feasible, but committing to drive silently when doing errands might be something that can be followed through on. This is not a competition.
6. Write each of the things you will do in the next week down, noting the modifications made for setting yourself up for success.
7. Over the course of the week, make a commitment to help yourself find calm, balance, or care using the Routes of Safety. You may find it useful to choose one to do each day, make a list of all five and check them off as you go, or use some other tool to remind yourself.

Adaptations

If you have dyslexia, dysgraphia, or a vision impairment, or do not enjoy doing writing-based exercises, you can download the audio file for the worksheet at http://www.passionandsoul.com/beloved.

Once you've downloaded it, you can answer the questions in a few different ways:

A. Write your answers on paper with your chosen writing instrument.
B. Type your answers out on your computer and save them for later.
C. Audio- or video-record your answers on a smartphone, computer, or other device.
D. Answer out loud.
E. Answer in your head.

Worksheet

Inner Guidance

1. _____

2. _____

3. _____

4. _____

Structure and Certainty

1. _____

2. _____

3. _____

4. _____

Sensory Experiences

1. _____

2. _____

3. _____

4. _____

Quality Relationships

1. _____

2. _____

3. _____

4. _____

Closeness and Proximity

1. _____

2. _____

3. _____

4. _____

Private Retreat

1. _____
2. _____
3. _____
4. _____

Protective Measures

1. _____
2. _____
3. _____
4. _____

Common Humanity

1. _____
2. _____

3. _____

4. _____

Going Forward

After a week, come back to the worksheet or reflect upon what the experience was like for you. Did any of the five Routes of Safety feel good to follow? Note those and consider working them in on a more regular basis.

If, at the end of the week, you were not able to explore all or even any of the Routes of Safety you set out to, be gentle. Do not use the word "should." This is not a competition and there is nothing wrong with having prioritized other things during the week of this exercise. Take a chance instead to reflect on the week and see if you did anything to show yourself care, find balance, or cultivate calm. No matter how the week has gone, remember to thank yourself for doing the work.

Chapter 12

WELCOME HOME: BEING YOUR OWN BELOVED FOR LIFE

You have known yourself for a long time.

You've known *you* since you were born, perhaps before. You were there when you scraped your knee for the first time and when you had your first kiss. You laughed out loud when you listened to hilarious jokes, and curled up like a ball when heartbreak came. Your heart swelled with pride when you accomplished something against all odds, and you spent time alone when you needed to think. Heartache, colds, fears, joy, delight, loss, delicious meals, perfect sunsets—you have been there for it all.

You alone are enough. You have nothing to prove to anybody. —Maya Angelou

BECOME YOUR OWN BELOVED

Even if the term "beloved" is not how you identify with yourself, you do have a relationship with you. You might be your own friend, associate, partner, journey-mate, companion, guide, ally, confidant, or soul mate. Either way, you are with you for life. Whichever way you think of yourself, connection is key—your connection to your Self.

It's easy to get lost in resources on how to care for ourselves, but as we have seen throughout this book, support and delight look different for every person. They will look different for you. But beyond that, we each get to practice that support and delight whether on our own or in partnership with others.

The care you seek can look like a lot of different things, based on what you want in your life. So, look at this list and see which ones you desire:

ease	rest	time
choice	curiosity	kindness
attention	patience	change
gentle	mindfulness	community
focus	slowing down	exploration
pleasure	awareness	acceptance
support	presence	comfort
joy	excitement	calm
contentment	happiness	serenity
delight	satisfaction	fun
indulgence	pride	ecstasy
enjoyment	bliss	satisfaction
agency	motivation	passion

Or is your call for something entirely different? This is your continued chance to find the you that you will delight in, thrive in, find peace in…or simply find *you* in.

This process is about coming home to you. Coming home to your Self.

> You are allowed to be both a masterpiece and a work in progress simultaneously. —Sophia Bush

The process does not end here. You get to keep building skills for delighting in your own company as long as you live. You get to keep doing the joy as well as the work you practiced in this book by:

- Following the Routes of Safety to help you feel grounded and connected (follow the work of Jake Ernst for more resources in this direction)
- Asking yourself questions (consider getting one of those "ask me anything" type of books for relationships and ask them of yourself, such as *Intellectual Foreplay: A Book of Questions for Lovers and Lovers-to-Be* by Eve and Steven Hogan)
- Using the various systems of love languages to show you that you matter (check out SelfLoveRainbow.com for playful tools great for all ages)
- Diving into your sensuality and body wisdom time and time again (*The Body Keeps the Score:*

Brain, Mind, and Body in the Healing of Trauma by Bessel van der Kolk is a great place to start)
- Enjoying your erotic Self (adrienne maree brown's *Pleasure Activism: The Politics of Feeling Good* and Betty Dodson's *Sex for One: The Joy of Selfloving* are both powerful works)
- Making and keeping promises and commitments to yourself (read Ayodeji Awosika's article, "How to Stop Breaking the Promises You Make to Yourself" to consider the topic further)
- Forgiving yourself and building self-worth when you are imperfectly, perfectly human (check out the TEDx Talk, "Cultivating Unconditional Self-Worth" by Adia Gooden)
- Connecting with yourself while being in relationship with others (explore the music, poetry, and spoken word of Lyla June and Supaman)
- Giving to community and having them give back to you (as well as relaxing into community—find more depth on this topic through *Rest Is Resistance* by Tricia Hersey)

And of course…taking yourself out on dates.

Welcome to the continued adventure of being authentic with your Self. This is a chance for a lifetime of delighting in self-connection. This is your opportunity to be your own beloved.

I believe in you.

Acknowledgments

I am so honored to have been able to work on this project as an act of self-love in and of itself. In 2009, when on a train from Chicago to New Orleans, I met Rose Fox, and my life was changed. They told me about the silver ring they wore, and it led me to the story I shared at the beginning of this book.

So first, thank you for letting me find my own wedding ring and go on my own journey.

Thank you so much to everyone who has helped me on this amazing book project over the years.

To my initial readers, friends, and Patreon supporters who have read pieces of this project as it evolved over time, from stand-alone essays and blog posts to what you hold in your hand today, your own sharing how this work changed you kept me fueled and allowed this work to change over time.

To my final readers, Inae Hwang, Ev Evnan, Averyn Salem, Razz Faeling, Dancing Spirit, and the members of Karada House (Mamana, Caritia, and René), your clarity, intimate sharing, love, and firmness in where course corrections needed to happen helped not just this book be better, but me as well. You are each gifts in my life.

To Dossie Easton, who amidst her own writing and life challenges gifted me with a truly touching foreword that shared from her own life. You continue to inspire me and generations of identity and erotic authenticity.

To my mother, whose trips to farmers markets modeled a beautiful act of self-love for me.

> Not everyone will understand your journey.
> That's fine. It's not their journey to make
> sense of. It's yours. —ZERO DEAN

To Ev, Hanna, Jordan, Master Cenna, Butterfly, Aiden, Hunter, Adam, Amy, Craig, Ava, Marshall, Jesse, Ayem, Glenn, Martin, and other partners and beloveds over the years who taught me that I needed to love myself, even when in relationships with others.

To friends who kicked my ass back into remembering who I am, as well as remembering to keep working on this project when it was being unpleasant to do.

To my therapists who asked me what my favorite color was.

To all the authors, artists, speakers, podcasters, musicians, teachers, and beautiful beings whose work on self-love, self-connection, self-compassion, and self-delight have inspired me over the years, especially Jake Ernst, who trusted me with publishing his work in print for its first time.

To my fantastic editors Elena Vega and Madeline Sturgeon who inspired me to take this further, helped me differentiate between passive and active voice, and, specifically Elena, took calls from me at random hours while believing in this project.

To the folks at Twin Flame, who trusted me enough to launch their imprint with my project.

And finally, to my *Self,* for doing the work and becoming my own beloved.

Much love to you all.

About the Author

Lee **Harrington** (he/they) is an internationally known spirituality, identity, relationships, and personal authenticity author and educator. He brings a combination of playful engagement and thoughtful academic dialogue to a broad audience, having taught classes, shared presentations, and delivered keynotes worldwide for over twenty years. An award-winning author and editor on gender, sexual, and sacred experience, his many books include *Traversing Gender: Understanding Transgender Realities*. He has been blogging online since 1998 and has been teaching since 2001. You can check out Lee's adventures, as well as his podcast, tour schedule, free essays, videos, and more, over at PassionAndSoul.com.

Made in the USA
Columbia, SC
14 September 2024